T0113363

PROBLEM DRINKING

How to Help a Friend

Charles Downs

Harold Shaw Publishers
Wheaton, Illinois

Library of Congress Cataloging-in-Publication Data
Downs, Charles.
  Problem drinking : how to help a friend / Charles Downs.
   p. cm. — (The Heart and hand series)
  Includes bibliographical references.
  ISBN 9780877886624
  1. Alcoholism. 2. Alcoholism—Psychological aspects.
3. Alcoholics—Rehabilitation. 4. Alcoholism—Religious
aspects—Christianity. I. Title. II. Series.
HV5035.D69 1990
362.29'27—dc20   90-8186
              CIP

99 98 97 96 95 94 93 92 91 90

146502721

I have said this to you,
that in me you may have peace.
In the world you will have tribulation;
but be of good cheer,
I have overcome the world.

—Jesus
John 16:33, RSV

Contents

Introduction

Alcohol is the most widely abused drug in our society, perhaps because it is legal and readily available. A leading cause of death, alcohol abuse takes the lives not only of problem drinkers, but also of innocent persons. More than 50 percent of all automobile accidents involve alcohol abuse. Drinking is also very prevalent in family violence. Abuse of alcohol can lead to alcoholism, a terrible disease that afflicts one in ten persons in our population without regard to gender, race, or social status. Even Christians become alcoholics. I know. I became an alcoholic, and I'm a minister.

But you probably didn't pick up this book because you are interested in alcohol statistics. You are reading this book because someone in your life has a drinking problem. That friend might be your spouse or offspring or some other family member. He might be a co-worker, employer, employee, or neighbor. Maybe your problem drinker is a close friend, a parishioner, or even your pastor.

Sometimes your friend drinks too much, and occasionally drinks at the wrong times. He drinks even though it is causing problems, and you've become concerned about the direction the whole thing is going. Very likely you haven't wanted to think of your friend as an alcoholic; the word sounds harsh and judgmental.

My first recollections of an alcoholic are of a neighbor in New York City where I grew up. His name was Henry. He lived with his wife and three children in an apartment, three houses away from my family. I was probably nine years old when I became aware of what was going on in that house. Henry's family was dirt-poor, and they raised a garden and chickens for food. The only time Henry worked was at Christmas, when he carried mail during the post office's seasonal rush.

On several occasions, the police were called because Henry was beating up his wife. He would be arrested, but he was always home again in a few days to take up where he left off. Once Henry's small children set a fire in a vacant lot. To teach them a lesson, Henry tried to put them into a heated oven. When a big fight with his wife ensued, he was arrested again.

The details are unclear, but sometime during my teenage years, Henry died from his alcoholism. His family moved away, and I have never heard of them again. His daughter, Nan, was close to my age. I often think about what she must have lived through, and I wonder if his two sons are now alcoholics. Little did I know then that I, too, would walk in Henry's footsteps.

Serious Questions

Why do people abuse alcohol, and how do they become alcoholics? Why do they continue to drink even when their drinking gets them into so much trouble? Can't they see what they're doing to themselves and to the people who love them? Why don't they stop drinking or at least control it better? What can you do to help someone you love stop drinking? What can you do to help yourself with all the craziness that his or her drinking brings into your life?

These are some of the questions this book addresses. The insights and suggestions come out of my own experience with alcoholism and recovery. I should also mention that, except for the stories in the first two chapters, the anecdotes in this book are true. To protect the people involved, I have blurred details and used fictitious names. My own story, however, is told as it happened.

Seed-Planting

When Jesus told the parable of the sower, he said,

"A farmer went out to sow his seed. As he was scattering the seed, some fell along the path; it was trampled on, and the birds of the air ate it up. Some fell on rock, and when it came up, the plants withered because they had no moisture. Other seed fell among thorns, which grew up with it and choked the plants. Still other seed fell on good soil. It came up and yielded a crop, a hundred times more than was sown."

When he said this, he called out, "He who has ears to hear, let him hear."

His disciples asked him what this parable meant. He said...
"This is the meaning of the parable: The seed is the word of God. Those along the path are the ones who hear, and then the devil comes and takes away the word from their hearts, so that they may not believe and be saved. Those on the rock are the ones who receive the word with joy when they hear it, but they have no root. They believe for a while, but in the time of testing they fall away. The seed that fell among thorns stands for those who hear, but as they go on their way they are choked by life's worries, riches and pleasures, and they do not mature. But the seed on good soil stands for those with a noble and good heart, who hear

the word, retain it, and by persevering produce a crop." Luke
8:5-10, 11-15

The good seed was the Word received in various ways by the
hearers. In some cases, it was rejected, in others it was welcomed.
The seed sprouted and grew, either to wither or to produce a harvest
of "a hundred fold."

I believe that God has called me to be a "sower of seeds," and
for the most part, I believe that the words you will read in this book
are "good seeds." I don't mean that I think they are Scripture, but
the ideas expressed have already demonstrated their viability in the
lives of many people. I pray that they might sprout, grow, and
produce a rich harvest in your life too. Because I know that each
person will receive them differently, just as Jesus knew that his
words would be so received, I must leave the result with God, for
it is only by his grace that we are healed.

A word about my use of gender language seems in order here. I
have referred to God in the male gender, not because I think that
God is a male, but because it still seems the best way to handle it.
Calling God "she" doesn't seem to be the answer, nor does using
the Word "God" redundantly in place of personal pronouns. I've
seen this done, and it seemed very cumbersome. "Them" is
theologically correct, but I'm not sure people are ready for that
either. So I refer to God as "Him" for the sake of simplified reading,
and not from a male chauvinist viewpoint.

In reference to alcoholics and to your alcoholic friend, I have
tried to use "he" in some cases and "she" in others, since alcoholics
come in both genders and from every station of life.

Charles Downs is not my real name. It will be obvious to you as
you read this book that I am a member of Alcoholics Anonymous.
AA has a policy that members ought to remain anonymous at
public-level media such as TV, radio, and published print. There

are two reasons for this. First, if a member announces membership to the world and then is found drunk, the world will notice and place AA's reputation at stake. At the same time, when a member uses sobriety and AA to gain notority, it can put a member's sobriety at risk.

The Alcoholics Anonymous World Services' Board of Directors, therefore, has requested that I publish this work anonymously. I gladly comply with their request. After all, this book isn't mine; it is God's.

I wish to express my gratitude to God, who has made my recovery possible, and who has given me this ministry.

I am also grateful for my friends and colleagues who have read this manuscript and made many helpful suggestions. Bill, Judy, Rick, Carolyn, Ted—thank you!

The two stories that follow are not "true" in the most literal sense, but nothing in them is false either! While not the actual stories of four real people, they are, nonetheless, true to life. They are based on accounts I have heard told by hundreds of people who were either alcoholics or friends or family members caught in an alcohol-soaked relationship. As you will also discover, these stories are reflective of my own experience as an alcoholic and drug addict, too.

As you read these stories, try not to be distracted by unfamiliar details. Everyone's story is different. The details of your alcohol-related experiences are probably unique to you. You may be tempted to compare these stories with your own. You may catch yourself saying, "My situation isn't that bad! Maybe I don't have a problem after all." Or, "Things are much worse for me than for the people in the stories."

Behind every alcoholic story is a set of dynamics and feelings that are common to them all. As you read these two stories—indeed, as you read the remainder of this book—try to identify with the underlying dynamics at work in your experience and the feelings that are similar to your own and to your friend's.

1
Jillian's Story

Jillian's alcoholic friend is her husband, Roger—at least they used to be friends. Although she probably wouldn't say it out loud, she actually felt more like a hostage. She also felt guilty about feeling trapped. Jillian and Roger had met twenty-eight years earlier during a young people's function at the Community Christian Church just outside of Kansas City. Jill had attended church most of her life and could not remember a time when she did not trust Christ as her Savior.

Jill could count on one hand the number of times she had seen her mother drink. She had to admit, however, that her father definitely had a drinking problem. Although he was a member of the church and held several positions of responsibility, he somehow managed to hide his drinking completely from anyone outside the family. He didn't drink every day, although he drank quite regularly. When he did drink, he never became violent or abusive. Actually he became rather mellow and lethargic. He usually withdrew from everyone and wanted to be left alone.

Jill never doubted her father's love for her. It was obvious that he cared very much for his daughter, and often there was warm closeness in their relationship. At the same time (usually when he was sober) he could be hostile and distant, punishing her for things that didn't make sense to her then or now. Jill had always loved her father and depended on the closeness, but she never really felt emotionally safe with him. She had been hurt too many times.

Jill felt the same way about God. She knew that God loved her and that she loved him. She often longed for a closer relationship with him but was intimidated by a haunting feeling that God would turn his anger upon her unexpectedly and inexplicably. She was also deeply confused and angry over God's apparently permissive attitude in letting her father get away with hiding his drinking from the church.

By contrast, Roger's parents were not Christians. His father was a daily drinker and openly alcoholic. He often came home from work drunk, and sometimes things got unpleasant. Roger often complained to his friend, John, about his father's drinking and the problems he was having at home. John, a member of the Community Christian Church's Youth Fellowship, had invited Roger to attend a social, thinking that supportive fellowship would be good for him. He hoped that Roger might find Jesus Christ as his true source of strength and help.

From the moment they met, Roger and Jillian were strongly attracted to one another. Roger accepted Jesus Christ as his Savior and vowed many times never to drink. For her part, Jill was grateful to God for sending her a young man who was as steadfastly opposed to drinking as she was. Jill and Roger talked often and long about these things, and in the process they fell in love; they were married four years after they first met.

At first, their marriage was wonderful, even though they struggled financially. Soon Jill and Roger had three children. Then Roger got a new position as a salesman with a pharmaceutical firm. Jillian always said that's when things took a bad turn. Six months after starting his new job, Roger came home one night with alcohol on his breath. He wasn't drunk by any stretch of the imagination, but it was obvious that he had been drinking. Jill panicked. "You've been drinking!" she screamed at him. "What about all your promises that you would never drink? How could you do this to me?"

"Look, honey," Roger said. "It's my job. We're pressured to drink. In the sales meetings and with customers, it is expected that we will drink. As a matter of fact, it has already been pointed out to me that if I *don't* drink at all, I'll find it difficult to get ahead. That's just the way it is."

"Then get another job!" Jillian shouted back.

"Jill, I like my job," he said. "I have a good chance for advancement. I really don't want to get another job."

"I see!" she said hotly. "You're putting your job and your drinking ahead of me. Already my needs come third in this marriage."

"Look," Roger said. The tone in his voice was beginning to change; he was losing patience with the discussion. "I don't intend to become like my dad or yours. I haven't forgotten what it was like for us, and I have no intention of becoming like that. I don't even like the taste of the stuff," he continued, "it's just something I have to do. I don't have to drink every day. I'm not going to drink every day. It's just once in a while, at sales meetings and with customers." His tone softened a little. "Look honey, I promise you it's going to be okay; just give me a break. You'll see."

Roger knew how to get his wife to give in. She didn't know what else to say. Jillian loved her husband very much and wanted to believe him. She was convinced that Roger wasn't going to change his mind about this. She also felt sure that something in their marriage died in that moment.

Jill hated it when he came home smelling like alcohol. Nevertheless, she argued with herself that his drinking was a necessary part of his job, that he didn't really like it, and that he was never going to become an alcoholic.

But Jill began to change her mind one Friday in July when Roger brought home a six-pack of beer. She got very angry with him, screaming about his drinking and pleading with him to stop. Roger explained that beer was a lot like soda and that it quenched thirst better than anything else he had ever tried. The weather was hot, and he had a lot of work to do outside, he explained. In the fight that followed, Jillian threatened to leave him if he didn't stop drinking.

Paradoxically, as his drinking became more frequent, Jillian continued to tell herself that drinking beer was not like drinking hard liquor and that Roger really would not become an alcoholic.

Once again Jill's illusions were shattered rather suddenly. She had been after her husband to repaint the bathroom, but it simply wasn't getting done. One day when he left on a three-day business trip, Jillian decided to do the job herself. She seldom poked around the basement and had no idea what was down there for paint and equipment. To her dismay, she found a bottle of vodka stashed away among the paint cans.

She never did get the bathroom painted. Instead, Jillian spent most of the next twenty-four hours crying and asking God, "Why are you letting this happen to me?" When her children saw her and asked why she was crying, she told them that she had discovered a bottle of vodka in the basement and that their father was becoming an alcoholic.

Jillian became angry—*very* angry! It occurred to her that there may be other bottles hidden in the house or the garage. A plan emerged in her mind. She undertook a thorough search of the house and garage. In all, she found eleven bottles of booze. She decided to line them all up on the kitchen counter in a prominent display.

When Roger returned from his business trip, he was greeted by a hostile, distant wife. Her only words were, "Go out into the kitchen and see what I found."

Roger went out and quickly returned. "Look honey," he started.

"I'm *not* your honey!" she stated flatly. "Your 'honey' is *alcohol*, and she's out in the kitchen. Go talk to her!" Jill burst out crying and ran upstairs to the spare bedroom. Roger returned to the kitchen, where he poured a glass of whiskey. After he drank it, he went upstairs to the bedroom to change his clothes. There he discovered that Jillian had moved all of her clothes out of their bedroom.

The cold war lasted for a week. As Jillian's anger cooled, she realized that family business required some sort of communication between her and Roger. She finally broke the silence by asking her husband to be honest enough to drink out in the open instead of hiding it in the basement or the garage. She also told him that she was not going to move back into his bedroom until he stopped drinking.

Although Jill had been attending church regularly and was involved in a number of the church's activities, Roger had become less and less involved as his drinking progressed. Until this time, he attended the Sunday morning worship service once or twice a month with Jillian. With this blow up, he stopped attending church altogether.

Jillian started staying away from church more now, too. People at church, including the pastor, had noticed that something was wrong. The pastor even came to see her once to try to get her to talk about her problems. But Jillian did not want anyone in the church to know that her husband was an alcoholic. She was too embarrassed to talk about it with anyone; she felt that real Christians shouldn't have this kind of problem.

Not talking about Roger's drinking meant hiding her pain. She knew that if she began telling the pastor or anyone else in the church about what was happening at home, the whole story would come gushing out. Almost overnight she became extremely critical of the pastor and aspects of the church's program. She never stopped attending church completely, but when she did attend she usually got angry because no one seemed to be showing an interest in her anymore.

Below the surface, Jillian seethed with anger toward God. She had always known that something like this was going to happen. She had loved God. She had wanted and needed a close relationship with him, and she was furious that this was how her devotion had been rewarded. Just like her father, God had taken advantage of their closeness to hurt her. So she stopped reading Scripture, and her only prayers were pleas that God would stop Roger from drinking. Although she would never have admitted it, she decided not to read the Bible or go to church regularly until God stopped her husband's drinking.

When Jillian asked Roger to stop hiding his drinking, he made a resolution. If she wanted him to drink openly, then he was going to. He also decided that she was going to be sorry that she moved out of their bedroom. Drink openly he did!

Roger drank more heavily, started drinking daily, and even started drinking in the morning. But whenever he drank, he *always* made sure that Jillian knew.

He started seeing other women. Jillian's first inkling came when she found a ticket stub from an adult movie house in the pocket of a pair of trousers she was taking to the cleaners. Then she found a sexually-explicit birthday card signed by someone named Andrea. Jill never said anything to him about the card; she had a feeling that he wanted her to find it.

Roger started having trouble at work. There were days that he couldn't make it to the office. He usually had Jillian call in sick for him. Finally, Jill received a phone call from her husband's boss; he told her that if Roger didn't do something about his drinking problem, he would lose his job.

"How ironic," Jill thought, "that he should be encouraged to drink as a part of his job and then be fired because of it."

The last of their children had just graduated from high school and had enlisted in the service. All three had been anxious to get away from home, just as Jillian and Roger had been in their youth. Now, alor ⌐ in the house with Roger, Jillian realized that she did not want to be married to him anymore. But she had no friends to talk to; nor did she have any means for supporting herself. She had never worked outside her home, and all of their possessions were in her husband's name. She didn't know if she could even get enough money together to retain an attorney.

Increasingly she started thinking about suicide. She remembered someone telling her a long time ago that anyone who commits suicide would go straight to hell. She doubted that hell could be any worse than what she was going through. It began to look like the only way out for her. At the same time, in a strange way, she started seeing suicide as a good way of getting even with Roger for the hell he was putting her through.

She only wished she could be there to see his face when he found her.

2

Doug's Story

Doug was born and raised in Brighton, Connecticut. His parents attended church occasionally but were not strong in either faith or commitment. On the other hand, Doug, from an early age, seemed possessed by the desire to find God. During his late teen years he responded to an invitation at a Billy Graham Crusade.

At the time, Doug was a student at Connecticut University, majoring in accounting and business. He was never really interested in the "party scene" on campus, but he had no problem with an occasional drink. He enjoyed a glass of beer once in a while. At times he would have a glass of wine with dinner, although he didn't really like wine very much. He might even have a mixed drink now and then at a social event.

But Doug couldn't understand why anyone would drink for the sake of drinking. As soon as he began to feel the effects of the alcohol, he was ready to quit. He could nurse a drink all evening, and he was not upset if alcohol was not being served at a particular event. He didn't care whether he drank or not.

His outlook and practice concerning alcohol didn't change much after he made his commitment to Christ. If he had difficulty understanding heavy drinking, he also had little tolerance for the small number of Christians in his circle of friends who were adamantly opposed to any use of alcohol by Christians. It seemed obvious to him that Jesus drank wine, as did the apostle Paul and other biblical characters. If the Bible taught anything on the subject, it taught moderation, not abstinence.

Doug's alcoholic friend was Gayle. He met her at the University. Doug was romantically attracted to her but quickly decided it would never work unless some changes were made. In the first place, she wasn't a Christian. Although a strong bond of friendship developed between them, Gayle wasn't interested in "that religious stuff." Doug invited her to attend church with him and also tried to get her to come for the campus's Christian group functions. All of these efforts were to no avail, though he never stopped trying. Doug also held back because of Gayle's drinking. From the time he met her, alcohol was a prominent part of her life.

But Doug was still strongly attracted to Gayle. His interest in her never waned, and somehow he had no desire to date other women. Because he could not see himself spending the rest of his life married to Gayle, he felt confused. His personal relationship with Jesus Christ stood at the very center and core of his life. How could he marry someone whose spiritual foundations were opposed to his own? If only he could get her to accept Christ! Somehow he hoped that he could change her.

Becoming a Christian might help her to stop drinking so much. Doug could plainly see that Gayle was headed for a disaster. He had seen her drunk many times in their years of friendship. On one occasion, for instance, Gayle had fallen behind in her schoolwork.

She had been warned that she wouldn't graduate if she didn't pull up her grades. She was given special assignments and a deadline date for their completion. As the deadline approached, Gayle had not even begun the projects. Doug kept pushing her to get the work done, and she kept insisting that she didn't have time to get to it. Finally, the day before the deadline, he insisted that she come over to his apartment so he could make certain she got it done. When she showed up, she had a bottle of wine with her.

"You're not going to drink *tonight,* are you?" he asked in disbelief.

"Doug," she replied, "I'm pretty shaky tonight. I haven't been feeling well today—I think I'm coming down with something. Besides, I'm under a lot of pressure to get this done. I'm only going to have one or two drinks to help clear my head and settle me down."

She drank the entire bottle of wine. When that was gone, much to Doug's consternation, she produced a pint of gin from her knapsack. Needless to say, she didn't get the work done. Doug did the projects instead!

She was too drunk to drive back to her place, so Doug let her sleep on his couch. The next morning, she was hung over badly. He drove her to her apartment, pushed her to clean up and change, and drove her to her professor's office to make certain the papers got turned in on time. He explained that she had been really ill, as the professor might plainly see, but that she had gotten the work done under great duress.

Then Doug took Gayle home and told her to go to bed. "I'll come over later this afternoon," he promised. "You owe me one, and you're going to listen to what I have to say to you whether you want to or not."

When he showed up at her apartment later that day, she looked a little better, but still was far from topnotch.

11

"Let's get this over with so I can go have a drink," she said.

"Go have a drink?" Doug asked in disbelief. "After last night, you're actually going to drink again tonight? I don't believe you! How can you keep on doing this to yourself?"

"Look, booze is the only stable thing in my life right now except for you, and sometimes I'm not too sure about you! A couple of drinks will help me to feel better."

"When did you ever stop with 'a couple' of drinks!" he retorted.

"So it gets out of hand sometimes. Big deal!" she shot back.

"Out of hand SOMETIMES? You almost didn't graduate because of your drinking! If I hadn't done the special assignments for you, you wouldn't have graduated this year. As it is, I'll bet that you have a hard time getting into grad school. Out of hand *sometimes*? You're going to lose your career."

"Well, I've been thinking about that," Gayle said. "I'm not sure that I want to pursue a career in business. There's a lot of pressure out there, and I'm having trouble just getting through college. If this is any indication of what the rest of my life is going to be like, forget it."

"The trouble you're having," Doug said in a rather fatherly tone, "is the amount you drink."

"I don't drink all that much," she replied. "Have you seen Pauline drink? She puts away lots more than I do."

"But I don't care how much Pauline drinks! I care about *you*. And I think you are an alcoholic!"

The word stung both Gayle and Doug. It was the first time he used the word, and he surprised himself by saying it.

"An *alcoholic*—you think I'm an alcoholic?" she shouted. "I can't be an alcoholic. An alcoholic is a dirty old man who wears a trench coat and a beat-up hat, hasn't shaved in six weeks, sleeps in cardboard boxes, and drinks Old Buzzard from a brown paper bag. I go to school, I hold down a part-time job, I wear nice clothes, and I drive a great car."

12

She paused.

"I'm *not* an alcoholic, Doug! I'm *not!* I can stop drinking anytime I want. I just choose not to right now. I enjoy drinking. Get off my case about it! OK? Understood?"

Doug felt sorry that he had accused her of being an alcoholic. Maybe she was right; maybe she wasn't. Maybe she *could* stop drinking. He wished she would want to stop. He could see only trouble for her if she kept on this way. And he still hoped they might get together someday—but not while she was like this.

On another occasion, Gayle called Doug collect one Monday morning at 6 o'clock. As nearly as she could tell, she was in Burlington, Vermont. She didn't know how she got there and had no idea where her car was. The last thing she remembered was driving to a bar a block from campus and having a couple of drinks. That was Saturday night.

Doug got the number of the payphone she was calling from, dressed, and drove over to the bar. Sure enough, her car was parked nearby. He called her back and told her that he would come up and get her after class. When he got to campus, he called her professors to get her assignments, telling them that she was out of town on a family emergency.

This sort of thing wasn't new. She had "misplaced" her car on several previous occasions while drinking, but she had always called him from her apartment when she came out of the black-out. This was the first time she had come out of a blackout somewhere else. Doug felt angry. He had other plans for the day, and he didn't want to drive all the way to Burlington and back just to get Gayle. But he felt obligated; he also felt responsible for her.

They didn't talk much on the way home. Doug was too angry. Gayle seemed really embarrassed by the whole incident. Within a few days, however, she was already joking about it.

It ceased to be funny two months later, when Gayle called Doug in hysterics. She had gone to see her physician because she had missed her monthly cycle twice. She was pregnant!

Doug had never had sex with her. Occasionally he wanted to and even thought she might be willing. But as a Christian, he knew he should not. He had often suspected her "indiscretions," but he didn't like to think about it very much. His suspicions were correct.

Doug felt sick. Gayle had become pregnant during a blackout and didn't remember anything about it, not even the man's name.

A couple of days later, Gayle was at Doug's place. "What am I going to *do?*" she moaned.

"I've been thinking," Doug said. "I can be the child's father."

"What are you talking about?" she asked.

"Getting married," he replied. "If we got married, everyone would think the baby is mine. I could be a good father to the child."

"Doug, you're so sweet—and I really care about you. But I'm confused right now. Let me think about it."

They never did talk about it. When he tried to bring it up, she put him off. Then, several weeks later, she showed up at his place saying the problem had been solved.

"Solved? What do you mean, 'solved?'" he asked. "How?"

"I got an abortion," she said, shrugging her shoulders.

Doug was dumbfounded. "I wish you had talked with me first. There had to have been some other way!"

"That's precisely why I didn't! I knew you wouldn't agree. Maybe *you* could have loved the child under these circumstances, but I couldn't. I know you care a lot about me, though I don't know why. I care about you, too. Sometimes I think I would like to be married to you. But we have too many differences. We have a great friendship. I don't want to mess it up by getting married—and I wasn't going to carry the baby full term so I could put it up for adoption. So there was only one answer."

"But Gayle," Doug began. *"Abortion!* That's like mur—"

"Shut up!" she interrupted. "I don't want to hear any of your Christian garbage. There was only *one* solution, and I did it. Now drop it! I don't want to discuss it anymore."

Gayle did graduate. She decided to sell real estate and was good at it. But she had to control her drinking strictly in order to make it. Even then, she often got herself into jams. Somehow she was able to make sales so the firm she worked for kept her on in spite of her problem.

Doug went on to complete graduate school. He got a job working for an accounting firm. He and Gayle saw each other often. He refused to date other women because he felt guilty whenever he did. Gayle continued her drinking and her occasional "indiscretions." She usually turned to Doug for help when she messed things up.

Doug felt trapped! He loved Gayle, yet he couldn't stand her. Often he tried to end their friendship, but he was unable to walk away from her. He wondered what people at his church would think if they knew what was going on.

How did he get himself into this? And how could he possibly get himself out?

3

Why Doesn't My Friend Stop Drinking?

It is probably obvious to you that your friend is self-destructing. You can see that your friend's troubles are the result of drinking. No doubt you have asked yourself many times, "Why doesn't he stop drinking—or at least cut down?"

I asked that question over and over in regard to my father. Dad was a daily drinker as far back as I can remember. He had a good job in New York City; he was the chief engineer for a company whose products are probably found in your kitchen. When his company was sold to a parent company in 1968, his drinking was dramatically changed. The company owners profited by millions of dollars, and Dad figured that the products *he* developed had made *them* rich and successful. His employers had profited handsomely, but all he got was a meager "thank you." He truly felt that he should have received a 7-digit bonus. That's when he "crawled into the bottle."

The most obvious results of my dad's drinking were the deterioration of his marriage and physical illness. I won't go into his attitude toward my mother here; suffice it to say that he became extremely difficult to live with. He also began suffering the visible signs of cirrhosis and alcoholic colitis. He often couldn't go to work for days at a time. There was little fear that he would lose his job, but there was great fear that he would lose his life. After a period of hospitalization, his physician told him that he would die if he didn't stop drinking.

Today, the medical community would have sent him to an alcohol treatment program. Back then he was sent home instead. Once home from the hospital, he quickly resumed his drinking. In six months he was hospitalized again. That time he died from final-stage cirrhosis. The year was 1972, and Dad was sixty-four years old.

During that period I kept asking myself, "Why does he keep doing this to himself? Why doesn't he stop drinking?" I even asked him once! He was angry at me for asking, but he told me that when a man gets older, he needs a little whiskey every day to help keep him "tuned up." "It keeps the blood circulating," he said.

I felt baffled and angry. I remember saying many times that I would *never* drink like Dad drank.

Today I know that he didn't stop drinking because *he couldn't!* And in spite of my good intentions, I came to the place where I couldn't stop drinking either.

What Is Alcoholism?

Alcoholism is addiction to alcohol. My father was addicted, and so am I. I say "am" even though I have not had a drink for many years (more about that later).

18

The American Medical Association has labelled alcoholism a disease, primarily because it has treatable physical symptoms. The dictionary defines *disease* as "any departure from health; any harmful or destructive condition." I certainly can't argue with the concept that alcoholism is a disease, using such a definition. But is alcoholism entirely a physical disease?

The United States Veteran's Administration, not wanting to pay millions of dollars in benefits to alcoholic veterans, argued before the Supreme Court in 1988 that, for its purposes, alcoholism is not a disease, but rather *willful misconduct*. Alcoholics *are* guilty of willful misconduct, I can't argue against that. But is alcoholism entirely a matter of choice?

In yet another direction, several Christian organizations, such as Substance Abusers Victorious and the Christian Alcoholic Rehabilitation Association argue that alcoholism is primarily *sin*. Certainly alcoholism arises out of human sinfulness. But is it entirely a spiritual matter?

I personally believe that a great disservice is done when alcoholism is pigeonholed into any of these categories in a mutually exclusive manner. Alcoholism involves all three! It is a spiritual, mental/emotional, and physical disease and cannot be understood or treated successfully unless all three dynamics are addressed.

Alcoholism as a Spiritual Disease

Swiss psychologist Carl Jung unsuccessfully treated a patient named Rowland H____ for alcoholism. After a serious relapse, Jung told Rowland that there was nothing more he could do, that Rowland was hopeless unless he had a genuine conversion experience.

Jung believed that each of us has a basic spiritual need and thirst which can only be satisfied by union with God. Jung said:

the evil principle prevailing in this world leads the unrecognized need into perdition, if it is not counteracted either by a real religious insight or by the protective wall of human community. An ordinary man, not protected by an action from above and isolated in society, cannot resist the power of evil, which is very aptly called the Devil.[1]

Rowland H____, according to Jung, was such a man when Jung knew him. In Jung's view, his craving for alcohol was a low-level substitute to satisfy his thirst for a union with God.

Sin, as I understand it, is rebellion against God. It is our doggedly stubborn resistance to God's will for our lives. We have a basic spiritual need that can only be satisfied by a relationship with God, whom we always seem to resist, often without taking notice of what we are doing. It is as though we are addicted to self-will. Perhaps this is the true expression of sin. The spiritual struggle which ensues manifests itself in many ways, of course. One of these is alcoholism.

I have not met an active alcoholic who isn't struggling mightily against God. In my experience, the alcoholic believes in God, even when unwilling to say so, and the alcoholic also believes in alcohol, but he or she prefers alcohol! Jung summed it up when he said to Bill Wilson, "Alcohol in Latin is *spiritus*, and you use the same word for the highest religious experience as well as for the most depraving poison. The helpful formula here *is spiritus contra spiritum*."[2] That is to say, for the alcoholic, alcohol and God are in conflict. Rebelling against God, an alcoholic chooses to fill the spiritual void by drinking.

Alcoholism as a Mental/Emotional Disease

In his book, *I'll Quit Tomorrow,* Vernon Johnson offers a helpful picture of how alcoholic drinking becomes the deeply willful act of a wounded mind.[3] He suggests that the alcoholic begins his drinking career at a near-normal emotional state. When he takes that very first drink, he feels *better.*

Before I continue with Johnson's picture, I want to disagree with his idea that alcoholics begin drinking at a normal emotional level. I seriously doubt that emotionally normal people start drinking to feel better. Many people don't like the way alcohol makes them feel. But people in emotional pain—those who live in dysfunctional families or who have suffered traumatic events—feel better when they drink. Perhaps they have suffered deep disappointments, or perhaps they are at risk emotionally, physically, or sexually. They often suffer from low self-esteem and insecurities. These people discover that alcohol makes them feel better. Depressed, angry, and anxious, they are trying to survive.

I've heard scores of recovering alcoholics relate the pain that led them to drink and the surprise relief that first drink afforded. Each said he had found what he'd been searching for: a way to feel better. So each drank a second time with the same result. Thus a pattern of trust was developed.

Therein lies the heart of willful alcoholic drinking: The alcoholic feels better when he drinks. "Alcohol can be trusted to make me feel better," is the mental process, whether conscious or subconscious.[4]

Back to Johnson's picture. The problem is that alcohol is a chemical depressant. Long-term use leads to a state of mental depression. So when the alcoholic begins drinking, he unknowingly sets a destructive process in motion. He starts drinking at a subnormal emotional level, feels better while drinking, then returns to his starting point after the effects of the alcohol have worn off. But in the course of time, his regular emotional level slips to a lower starting point—the point to which the alcoholic will return after the alcohol has worn off—the point from which he drinks again "to feel better." At the same time, the level of "high" experienced during drinking keeps slipping commensurately lower.

Over a period of years, the emotional level of the alcoholic slides into deep depression. From then on the alcoholic drinks to feel better. The feeling of "better" becomes much less pleasant than it was in the beginning. But to the alcoholic it is, nonetheless, better! The alcoholic always feels better when he drinks and doesn't understand why he feels so much worse when not drinking.

So the alcoholic chooses willfully and consciously to drink. When your friend feels terrible—when alcohol is the only thing he's found to make him feel better—he drinks! And it doesn't matter how bad "better" is; it's better than feeling terrible.

Alcoholism as a Physical Disease

When I speak of alcoholism as a physical disease I am not speaking of the physical symptoms that result from abusive drinking, but rather of the process by which a person becomes physically addicted to alcohol. A physical addiction involves a biological dependence on a chemical substance. When the chemical is withdrawn, adverse physiological symptoms appear, such as trembling, sweats, and hallucinations.

There is still great mystery surrounding the question of alcoholism as a disease, and all the facts will likely not be known for many, many years. We do know that alcohol is a highly addictive substance, and that drinking it heavily over a period of time will lead to a physical addiction in which the body's organs become dependent on alcohol for "normal" functioning.

An idea that is gaining popularity these days is the notion that alcoholism is an inherited disease. In 1985, *Alcoholism: An Inherited Disease,* published by the U.S. Department of Health And Human Services, reported the findings of a study designed to answer the question of why alcoholism seems to "run in families."

The studies involved children of non-alcoholic parents who were adopted at birth by alcoholics, children of alcoholics who were adopted at birth by non-alcoholics, animal studies, and a host of other creative approaches. The report is highly technical, but it concludes that there is probably a genetic predisposition to alcohol addiction (and a number of other drugs) which follows biological lines. In simple language, the study concluded that when a person who is born with a genetic predisposition to addiction abuses alcohol or drugs sufficiently, addiction is much more likely to result.

We also know that long-term heavy drinking will lead to an addiction. The amount of time and alcohol required varies a great deal. I've known people who had to drink heavily for many, many years before they crossed the invisible line of addiction. This, I think, is what happened to my father.

Again, I am convinced that alcoholism is not attributable only to physical or to mental/emotional or to spiritual disease alone; it is a constellation of all of them. Alcoholism is a disease of spirit, mind, and body. It is generated by a three-layered addiction; and persons who are so afflicted suffer spiritual, mental, and physical damage.

My Story

It's easy to trace the disease, dependency, and damages in all three of these areas in my story of alcoholism.

My parents, who had been married since 1932, had my brother in 1935. I was born in 1937 on Boston's North Shore. When I was ten months old, my father got a new job in New York City. My earliest memories go back to 1940. Those memories do not include alcohol being used in my home, but sometime during the next ten years, it became a constant presence and a powerful influence. By the time I was eleven, there were always cases of beer around, a cabinet full of hard liquor, and several bottles of wine.

My father usually had two or three drinks when he came home from work. During the evening he would have many beers. My mother would join him in drinking, but she often expressed her fear that he would become an alcoholic. Every social event centered in drinking. All of our relatives and friends drank; some of them drank constantly, or so it seemed.

My mother was rarely drunk. But my father got drunk all too frequently. Looking back, I realize that with such early, consistent exposure, it would have been strange if I *hadn't* been interested in alcohol.

I first drank when I was twelve years old. My parents went out for the evening, forgetting to lock the liquor cabinet. I had heard of a drink called "The Zombie," and I determined to make one. I had no idea what was in it except that it was made from 151 proof rum. The drink I concocted tasted terrible, but I drank it anyway. Then I tried to make another drink that would taste better, using different ingredients. The second drink tasted no better than the first; but again, I drank it anyway. These, I might quickly add, were large drinks made entirely from hard liquors.

After half an hour my father came home. I knew that he would smell the alcohol on my breath, so I tried to go up to my room. But I couldn't stand up! I ended up crawling up the stairs. I fell asleep quickly, but awoke shortly with a bad case of the "bed-spins." I needed to vomit. With difficulty, I made my way to the bathroom and back to bed. No sooner had I gotten back in bed when I had to vomit again. Again I made it to the bathroom and back, but I was continuing to get drunker. By the time I had to vomit yet again, I could not even get out of bed. I vomited on the floor after that. I don't think my parents ever found out I'd been drinking. My mother simply assumed that I had been sick in the night. I *had* been sick—no doubt about that. But I was not about to reveal the true nature of my sickness.

I don't really know how much I drank during the course of the next eight years, but I drank every time I could. While some of my drinking was probably due to peer pressure, much of it was due to my developing psychological and spiritual dependency on alcohol. Also, drinking had been modeled by every adult in my immediate and extended family. "Adults drink" was a clear message. As I grew toward adulthood, I adopted the ways of adults around me.

Sometime in my early teens my parents stopped going to church. By my teenage years I didn't know if there was a God. I had been told that there was a God, and the Bible was wielded as a weapon to make me tell the truth about my secret activities. But I felt certain that God was primarily a punishing God, and I feared death desperately. Somehow I equated dying with falling asleep, so from the time I was twelve, I suffered from a sleep disorder.

I learned from an early age to hide my feelings and never felt safe sharing emotions with anyone. I felt no emotional support whatsoever. I can't remember anyone saying, "I love you," when I was growing up. To this day ghosts of the past tell me I am no good, that there is something wrong with people who believe in God and refuse to drink.

Interestingly enough, I remember getting down on my knees one night when I was thirteen. Alone and in the dark of my bedroom I asked God to show himself to me if he was real. I occasionally attended church during my teenage years and often listened to radio preachers, but nothing made sense to me.

After graduation from high school I attended classes at an aviation school in New York. I wanted to be a flight engineer—one of my grandiose ideas. After six months of classes, I flunked out because I couldn't handle the math. From there I got a job as a machinist in an aircraft jet engine plant on Long Island. After a short time, I was laid off because the company was in the process of going bankrupt. I seemed to be ruining everything I touched. I was convinced that my family was right—I would never amount to anything.

My only alternative seemed to be military service, and so I joined the Air Force. During the waiting period before my departure for boot camp, my uncle invited me to go to New Hampshire with him on a job. There I met a family who knew Christ. I went to church with them and heard the gospel as I had never heard it before. An invitation was given; I didn't respond to it publicly, but I did privately! I asked Jesus into my life, and from that moment I sensed a deep change within. However, I felt I could not talk about it at home.

I returned to New Hampshire many times in the next few weeks. People in that church began telling me that God might be calling me into the ministry. That seemed as unlikely an idea as any I had ever heard. In and out of trouble regularly, I was a juvenile delinquent, an urban terrorist. Besides, the Air Force had an option on my life for the next four years. I was twenty years old.

To make a long story short, the Air Force deferred me because of a prior physical condition, asthma. I had no alternative! Ministry, as a calling, was put in front of me. It was my only choice. Now I realize there has never been any other choice for me. But the road to that knowledge has been long and hard.

I have heard about people who were delivered immediately from the grip of addiction when they were converted. That didn't happen for me. My progression into alcoholism and drug addiction was not halted by either my conversion or the call to ministry. Perhaps I would not have sunk into alcoholism if I had not been in spiritual rebellion against God.

I began preparing for the ministry by enrolling in a Christian college in New England. There I met Jean during my freshman year. We began seeing each other regularly, fell in love, and married two years later. Her background was far different from mine. In her Christian home, no one smoked or drank. Jean didn't know what she was getting in for when she said, "I do." During our early years together, she was displeased to discover that I smoked and was angry and tearful whenever I drank. I didn't drink a lot, but I always wanted to drink more. I didn't like Jean's reaction.

Our small denomination didn't require a seminary education for ordination. I attended seminary later when we switched denominations. After college, I was called to my first church. From the very beginning, I really did not want to be in the ministry. During my first pastorate, I began trying to change careers. I spent countless hours attempting to get into another line of work, or at least into a church where I might be happier. Except for a brief period, God never allowed me to do anything other than pastoral ministry. (And that brief period involved a business partnership in a publishing business, which ended in disaster.)

Because I wasn't happy in the work of ministry, I tried to find that elusive happiness by changing churches. I blamed my problems on whatever church I was in at the time, and always believed that things would be different in the next church.

A rather blunt riddle asks, "If you crate up a donkey in New York and ship it to California, what do you have when you uncrate it in

Los Angeles?" The answer is obvious. Geographic cures don't work. My problems went with me. Wherever I went, there I was! I didn't change any during the trip. When I arrived at each new church, I was still in rebellion against God's calling for my life. It finally came to the point where God even blocked my moving. I pleaded, begged, bargained, cajoled, and raged—all to no avail. Interestingly enough, on one occasion, while fundamentally rejecting the ministry as my life's work, I grandiosely pursued placement in a large, prestigious church. I was shattered when my executive minister told me that he couldn't put my name before their search committee because they would be looking for someone "with a different track," as he put it.

I also completed work on a D.Min. program. When I received the degree, it occurred to me that I now had the "terminal degree" in a field where I didn't want to be. So I celebrated with a five-month depression.

My deep-seated resentment against God grew until it filled my life. (Ironically, I recently encountered a man who was my roommate in college. He was carrying an equally large resentment against God because he wanted to go into the ministry but has never been allowed to do so.) In the end, my resentment against God took on an added dimension because, as a minister, I could not pursue my drinking as I would have liked. *Spiritus contra spiritum.*

I suspect that I was born with a genetic predisposition to addiction. Louis, a recovering alcoholic, said something to me early in my recovery that helped me greatly. I was still denying the seriousness of my problem at that point. He said, "Ray, if you ate liver and onions for the first time at age twelve, the age you took your first drink, and you vomited violently from it, would you have ever eaten it again?"

"Probably not," I replied.

"Then why do you think you continued to drink?" he queried.

"I don't know."

"Because you *had* to. You're addicted to alcohol!"

Louis was correct. Because I grew up in an alcohol-soaked environment—bottles of liquor always present in my home and parents who drank—I was destined to take that first drink. I can see the progression clearly. I always thought about alcohol—even as a small child—and I always returned to it.

During the years at my first church, I discovered an answer to the dilemma of Jean's displeasure over my drinking. Because our church was small, I found other employment to make ends meet. Working as an orderly in a hospital, I discovered that tranquilizers and narcotic pain killers *made me feel better* without the dreaded reaction from Jean. From then on I used these drugs as a substitute whenever it was inconvenient to drink.

Over the years that followed, there was less and less time between periods of drinking and more and more alcohol consumed during them. Then I started getting drunk unintentionally.

Once, for instance, a repairman (who happened to attend worship at the church I served) was coming to the church to work on the sound system. At 10:00 in the morning I was feeling shaky, so I decided to take "just one drink" to steady myself. When the man arrived at 1:00, I was thoroughly drunk. He helped me stagger to the sanctuary where I lay down on a pew. I was too drunk to speak or even to stand up!

I planned on having only one drink. But as soon as I had that drink, I had to keep on drinking until I was drunk. I figured then that I was in deep trouble, that I would lose my position because of that fiasco. But it turned out that the service person was also an alcoholic. It came as no shock to him to see the local minister drunk in the early afternoon. He never said a word to anyone, because I never heard about it—and I surely would have, had he told!

Not once did I consider giving up drinking. That wasn't the problem, as I saw it. The problem was how to control my drinking

29

better so that embarrassing situations wouldn't happen again. After that, I managed to make it through each day without a drink—often with the help of tranquilizers or narcotic pain killers—but at night I knew I could drink without getting caught.

In 1979 my brother died from cancer of the liver. Frankly, I was afraid. Like me, he was a heavy drinker, and I knew heavy drinking does severe damage to the liver. I was drinking a lot and getting sick a lot. It was a miracle if I could go two or three days without drinking. Because of my terror, I somehow stopped drinking for over two years. The potential problems were beginning to outweigh the benefits.

I need to add here that, at the time, I *liked* drinking. I was in a profession I didn't want to be in, serving churches I didn't want to be serving. I was severely depressed. So, in spite of the frequent hangovers and shaking, in spite of nearly getting caught on several occasions, I drank to feel better. In *Twelve Steps and Twelve Traditions*, Bill Wilson writes, "We drank for the temporary comfort of oblivion."[5] That describes my actions exactly. During that period of drinking, I was able to achieve an unbelievably euphoric state. All my feelings were numbed by the chemical effects of alcohol, and I felt better. I not only *had* to drink, I *wanted* to drink. I missed the "temporary comfort of oblivion."

During the two years of my abstinence I moved to another church. Jean and I were having a terrible time with one of our teenagers. Instead of supporting us, several people in the church turned against us, claiming that I was not a fit pastor since I could not control my teenager. That position became my all-time worst pastoral experience. So I changed denominations and was immediately hired to plant a new church for my new denomination in that same town.

The pressure to succeed was great, but I was not succeeding! How I missed the "temporary comfort of oblivion." Alcohol called, but I was still too scared to respond. Then I read Eric Bern's book, *The Games People Play.* To my delight, one of the games was called "Alcoholic." According to Bern, there is no such thing as an alcoholic. It is only a game people play. The payoff is guilt (God knew that I had plenty of that!). If, through counseling, the "alcoholic" can be freed of the need to feel guilty, he would be able to drink normally. I saw a glimmer of hope, and responded by getting my version of "counseling." I took a quarter of Clinical Pastoral Education (CPE) at a nearby state mental hospital. When it was over, I declared myself "cured."

During this same period, I read a book by a physician on preventing a heart attack, something I was also becoming concerned about. His advice was not to worry about being twenty-five pounds overweight (which I was), exercise at least three times a week (well . . .), take an aspirin a day (which I did), and *take one or two drinks daily* (which I very much wanted to do—one or two *big* drinks!). I became convinced that I could drink safely once again. I expected to "feel better" and control my drinking so that I could "take it or leave it," as they say.

So during the summer I began planning to drink again on Christmas day. And I did. On Christmas day I had two glasses of wine. It was *wonderful!* I didn't drink again for another week, and I was certain that I was cured. You can't imagine my surprise when, within a very short span, I went back to drinking until I was drunk and sick just as I did when I stopped in 1979. I couldn't figure out how that could have happened. According to the books I'd read, there wasn't any such thing as an alcoholic, was there? And I was cured, wasn't I? So why did I drink every night? Why couldn't I stop even for a day or two? Why was I getting sick every morning again? I couldn't even control my drinking. Why did I drink when I didn't want to?

It was as though I had stepped out of an airplane without a parachute. I was in free-fall, yet I still wanted to drink. I often said that I could never imagine myself as a "non-drinker." But something was different. There was no more euphoric state. Every night I started drinking at 8:00 or 9:00 P.M., and I drank until I passed out, the only "temporary comfort of oblivion" I could attain. At first, I passed out by 1:00 A.M. But with the progression of my alcoholism, I couldn't reach oblivion until 4:00 or later.

I didn't realize I was in a deep depression. For me, one of the components of depression is anxiety, and my anxiety level was sky-high. During the day, I directed my energy level into "doing." I could literally out-work five or six people. No one wanted to work for me, and I don't think my family wanted me around because of my work level and my expectations of others.

But then I couldn't get to sleep at night. The only way I could calm down enough was to drink until I passed out. In effect, I anesthetized my anxiety with alcohol. I remember being told by a physician years before, as he handed me a prescription for valium, that wine was a better tranquilizer—"a natural tranquilizer." For me, that helped to legitimize my drinking. But in tranquilizing my anxiety, I was deepening my depression, because alcohol is a chemical depressant. So as I slipped deeper and deeper into depression, my anxiety level went higher and higher, requiring more and more alcohol to achieve the desired result.

During the last year of my drinking, I slept no more than five hours a night. I awoke with a terrible migraine headache to go with the hangover. One night my wife woke me up because I was grinding my teeth fiercely and she was concerned that I would break a tooth. My mouth hurt for days afterward. Soon I slept only four hours a night, then three, then two. Most nights I slept in the family room. Jean and I were drifting apart, and my daughter was deeply upset about it.

Another symptom of my high anxiety was extreme and irrational fear. I had become convinced, for instance, that there was an evil spirit living in the ladies' room in the church basement. Being a Christian and the spiritual giant that I was, I felt certain it was after me. Unfortunately, there were times when I had to be alone in the church basement. Such times were filled with fear. On many occasions, I literally ran from the church in terror.

Looking back, it seems ridiculous. But that is where alcohol brought me. I was, indeed, in free-fall. And, inevitably, I crashed.

A Threefold Addiction

Alcoholism, then, in my view, is multi-layered, involving *spiritual addiction*—an addiction to self-will that causes us to resist the will and presence of God (in other words, *sin!*); *psychological addiction*—a conscious dependence on alcohol to help us cope with daily living; and *physical addiction*—the condition in which the organs of the body have adapted to an alcohol-soaked environment and require the presence of alcohol to function "normally." Where there is a conjunction of these elements, alcoholism will occur.

Unfortunately, Christians are not immune to the trap of alcoholism. A friend who is a member and respected leader of a church in a nearby town recently dropped by my office to chat. During the course of the conversation he revealed that he was struggling with drinking. I had never mentioned my own struggles, but he had pieced it together from things I had said. I never would have guessed that he was having such a problem himself. I suspect that there are others like him in every church.

Christians may have a difficult time accepting the idea that true converts to Jesus Christ could suffer from a spiritual addiction to alcohol. But we need to remember that we are saved *sinners*—nothing more, nothing less. We are saved in spite of our sinful natures, and we will never be free of our sinfulness until we see the Savior face to face. It is one thing to have saving faith; it is quite another to turn our lives and wills over to the care of God *in everything*. Who among us can claim such an achievement? Sooner or later, every Christian struggles with surrendering to the will of God over the protests of his or her self-will. For the alcoholic Christian, however, the struggle is much more difficult. In many cases the battle seems to have been lost, at least to outward appearances.

But there's a reason for this—and that's what we'll be discussing in the next chapter.

Notes
1. *Pass It On* (New York: Alcoholics Anonymous World Services, Inc., 1984), pp. 381-386. Reprinted by permission.
2. Ibid.
3. Vernon Johnson, *I'll Quit Tomorrow* (San Francisco: Harper and Row, 1980), pp. 8-34.
4. Ibid.
5. Bill Wilson, *Twelve Steps and Twelve Traditions* (New York: Alcoholics Anonymous World Services, Inc., 1984), p. 120. Reprinted by permission.

4

My Friend Is Acting Strange . . .

Alcoholism has some unmistakable symptoms. The primary one, of course, is drinking. Perhaps this sounds like a strange statement, but I'm quite serious. Every active alcoholic drinks.

The drinking may be done openly, as in Manny's case. He told me that he had recently looked through the family photo album, and it struck him that he is holding a can of beer or a mixed drink *in every picture* of him from age eighteen until he began his recovery in his early forties.

Or the drinking may be done in secret, as in my case. Although drinking was not acceptable, either to my wife or her family or to my church, I needed to drink. So I did what I had to do—I hid as much of it as I could. Increasingly, however, evidence of extensive drinking became visible in spite of my best efforts.

Once, in a vain moment during my birthday party, I showed my "wine collection" to some of my guests. I had built a secret room in the basement of the parsonage where I stored cases and cases of wine along with dozens of bottles of whiskeys. A friend, rather than being impressed, responded, "Wow, Charles, you must drink a *lot.*"

Done openly or under cover, drinking is the primary symptom of alcoholism.

Another symptom is the diagnosable package of physical ills that occur because of alcohol's toxic effects on the organs of the body. I only mention this in passing because, while worth noting here, it does not bear upon the main thrust of this book. There are many books that present the data far better than I could. Several are listed in the resource section of this book.

For our purposes, the other important symptom is the alcoholic's baffling and confusing change in personality and behavior.

As I sat down at the computer to begin work on this chapter, the telephone rang. The caller was a woman I know. Her daughter, now in her late twenties, had been arrested in a nearby town the night before on a charge of drunk and disorderly conduct. Her daughter had to appear in court that morning, and the woman was calling to ask me for suggestions in handling the situation. In the course of the conversation, she said her daughter had always been pleasant, talented, and energetic. After nearly ten years of drinking, however, her personality was changing for the worse. "What is happening to my daughter?" my friend asked me desperately.

What is happening to her happens to every alcoholic. The details of each alcoholic's story may be different from anyone else's, but there is a set of underlying dynamics that is uniform for everyone addicted to alcohol. Let's explore the pattern.

Acquiring and Using Alcohol

Several years ago I watched a TV interview with a very famous entertainment personality. The interviewer asked, "What situation causes you the greatest panic?" Without missing a beat, the entertainer said, "Running out of beer on Sunday." Everyone laughed. I don't know if he was joking or not; for the alcoholic, being out of alcohol is the worst of all scenarios. As psychological and physical addictions progress, the alcoholic experiences an ever-increasing preoccupation with drinking.

Because of the physical addiction, when the alcoholic does not drink, withdrawal symptoms appear. In the average, mid-stage alcoholic, the main symptom is "the shakes." The shakes are terrible. In my case, every nerve ending in my body seemed to be on fire. I physically shook (thus the name) and found it impossible to do much of anything. In the late-stage alcoholic, delirium tremors (DTs) will develop. The DTs are frightening; the alcoholic has terrifying hallucinations.

Meanwhile, at the psychological level, the alcoholic has learned that when she feels bad emotionally, drinking works to make her feel better every time. As the disease progresses, she feels progressively worse emotionally between drinks because of alcohol's depressive qualities. The alcoholic slips deeper and deeper into depression. When the "normal" emotional base becomes more and more painful, *the only thing that works is drinking.* Getting and using alcohol becomes the center of the alcoholic's life. Eventually, she will become willing to do almost anything to get and use alcohol, even when it conflicts with her values. At this level, the misbehavior includes lying, cheating, stealing, manipulating people and circumstances, and irresponsibility at home, at work, and in other obligations. All the while, the alcoholic will adamantly deny that drinking is a problem.

Lowered Inhibitions

Ethyl alcohol is an anesthetic closely related to ether. It acts on the central nervous system by depressing the brain's electro-chemical activity in a descending fashion from the cortex (the surface) to the medulla (the base).

Of all people, perhaps Christians understand best that there is a lower nature at work in each of us. Even the apostle Paul wrote of his inward struggle against his own lower nature in Romans, chapter seven. Under alcohol's influence, people think about doing things they would never do when sober, things that are motivated by sin. According to experts, self-control comes from the function of the cortex where the value system is "stored." As the function of the cortex is depressed, thinking and judgment are impaired. Inhibitions and self-regulation are lowered.

Thus, while lying, stealing, manipulating, and shirking responsibilities to get and use alcohol, the alcoholic also engages in behavior that is socially unacceptable, often morally wrong, and sometimes even illegal. Tragically, the people most deeply scarred by the active alcoholic's behavior are the people she loves the most.

Blackouts

Blackouts are a strange phenomenon in which, for reasons not yet entirely known to science, information is not stored by the brain for future retrieval. It's like typing several pages of information into a computer, then turning it off without saving the information. When the computer is turned on again, the information is not on the disk and cannot be retrieved.

In a blackout, the alcoholic goes about his business (including the patterns of lying, stealing, manipulating, and irresponsible actions) as usual. But when he "wakes up," he remembers none of it. Jimmy, a blue-collar worker living in a Northeastern state, left work one afternoon and "stopped off" for a few beers. He immediately went into a blackout. He woke up the next day at the top of a 100-foot water tower in a neighboring state. He has no idea how he got there.

Ed, a Christian and a leader in his church, routinely wakes up in bed with women he doesn't even know.

Margaret, a young single woman, has two children. She has no idea who their fathers might be and no recollection of their conception.

I have talked with many prison inmates who have been convicted of crimes they do not remember committing. One of these, John, told me that when he woke up, he was in jail. He had killed his wife while in a blackout. He has no memory of the murder whatsoever.

More often, blackouts involve misplacing cars (like Gayle in Doug's story) and forgetting information and commitments. They can last a few moments or a few weeks. Edith took a trip to France with her husband, and although she has pictures of herself in Paris, she has no memory of the trip, not even of traveling to or from Europe.

Repression

Dr. Vernon Johnson, in his book *I'll Quit Tomorrow*, describes the process of repression as it affects the active alcoholic. There is a high emotional price to be paid when the alcoholic lies, steals, cheats, manipulates people and responsibilities, hurts his loved ones emotionally or physically, and engages in negative behaviors.[1]

When compelled and controlled by alcohol, the alcoholic does things that are in direct conflict with his values and standards. This misbehavior creates great inward stress. The alcoholic experiences high levels of guilt feelings and emotional pain because of his actions. To relieve the pain, the alcoholic drinks more—thus setting the stage for yet more alcoholic behavior. As the emotional pain intensifies, he deals with the situation by denying that his behavior has any real meaning or that it truly harms himself or others.

The normal person controls his behavior with standards and values. But the alcoholic's behavior is controlled by alcohol. The only solution is to bring standards and values into line with the behavior. I recently saw a bumper sticker that said, "When all else fails, lower your standards." The problem is that we can't—not really! Subconsciously we are very aware of the difference between right and wrong. Because of this tension between his values and what an alcoholic actually does, the end product is someone in extreme inward pain and totally out of touch with the reality of his own actions. Drunk driving is a good example of this.

Howard is an alcoholic who uses his car to go where he can buy and drink alcohol. Because he drives while drunk, he has had a series of car accidents. Howard has "totalled" five cars to date, and he has had a serious accident in which he killed a pedestrian. He is unable to get car insurance, and now his driver's license has been permanently revoked.

One might think that Howard would realize the seriousness of what he has done, but he is totally out of touch with the reality of it. He was sent to a special school and given a jail term. Now that he has "paid his debt to society," Howard has resumed his routine as though nothing had happened. He owns a car, and although he has no license, no insurance, and no registration, he drives to places where he can get and use alcohol. Then, when he is drunk, he drives home.

Recently, in a nearby town, a pickup truck collided at a high rate of speed with an ambulance. Everyone in the ambulance was killed: the eighteen-year-old trainee driver, the elderly patient who was being transported for dialysis, and the attendants. So was the driver of the pickup, who was driving drunk—and without a license. It had been suspended as a result of a previous drunk-driving arrest!

Violent family behavior is another example of what happens when alcoholics repress their drinking problem. Gerri's family spent several hours preparing a special meal for her father's birthday. Gerri, who was in elementary school, went to a friend's home to get a homework assignment. When she arrived back home, her father was already there—and furious that she was two minutes late. When the little girl walked in, he exploded at her for being late and for ruining his birthday. He picked up his plate full of food and threw it at the wall. Then he walked out and got drunk.

Damaged Limbic System

As if all of this weren't enough, long-term alcohol use does physiological damage to the brain's limbic system where emotional functioning takes place. Continued abuse leads to a state of deep clinical depression. As the alcoholism progresses, so does the depression, and the alcoholic becomes more and more dysfunctional. Because her outlook is depressed, life becomes overwhelming. Normal daily problems and situations become terrible burdens, and life's hard knocks become impossible to deal with.

Negative emotions come to the front. The alcoholic's personality, in time, is dominated by fear, resentments, and punishing. She is loaded down with self-pity, and the only apparent solution is to have another drink.

Many alcoholics have, at one time or another, found themselves on a psychiatrist's couch. There are many fine psychiatrists who have an understanding of addictions. Unfortunately, many do not. Some (should I say it?) may even be alcoholics themselves. In many cases, psychiatrists who are unaware of the addiction in their patient may treat only the *depression* (by prescribing mind-altering drugs that act synergistically with alcohol) and not the real root problem—the alcoholism itself.

Ellen was institutionalized off and on for many years for depression and was on several psycho-tropic drugs during this period. She had become an alcoholic as a young woman in college. Her parents sent her to see a psychiatrist, but her depressive condition worsened. Meanwhile, she drank alcoholically whenever she could. One day, after being released from a stay in a psychiatric hospital, she encountered a former college friend. Her friend, now in recovery from alcoholism, told her that alcohol might be the real problem. No one had ever suggested that to Ellen before. Her friend offered to take her to an Alcoholics Anonymous meeting. Ellen accepted! Today, she is in her tenth year of sobriety and has no signs of the clinical depression which her psychiatrist once diagnosed as "hopeless."

Spiritual Rebellion

It is easy to see from what I've already said about the alcoholic that he is physically and mentally sick as a result of alcohol abuse. It should be no surprise that he is spiritually sick as well.

I agree with the long-standing idea that every human being has a spiritual longing for the presence of God. Each person also has a sin-nature that pushes God away. We want God, but we do not want to submit to God's lordship or leadership. The struggle between these opposing forces becomes very intense in active alcoholics. Almost without exception, God is a sore subject. Driven to get and drink alcohol, confronted before God—even if entirely at the subconscious level—of wrongful behavior, and filled with guilt and depression, every alcoholic I know is engaged in a spiritual struggle against God. As I see it, this rebellion takes one of three possible forms. For some, their rebellion is a strange mixture of all three.

The first form of spiritual rebellion is that of functional atheism. When I met Ted, he was new to sobriety, very intelligent, and a one-time Christian who had since been "enlightened." According to Ted, there was no God and no need for one. At the same time, Ted loved the Scriptures. He seemed unaware of the paradox he exhibited: he could defend inspiration and literal interpretation of the Bible in one breath and deny the existence of God in the next without connecting the two. As his sobriety stabilized, and with some guidance, he was able to approach his spiritual dilemma more clearly. After recommitting himself to the Lord, he admitted that he had always believed in God but had felt condemned before God because of his alcoholic behavior. Because he could not stop drinking, his only option was to get rid of God. He did this by waging daily warfare. Ted was in a constant battle to convince himself that God didn't exist. If God didn't exist, Ted would be off the hook. But of course, he couldn't get rid of God. None of us can!

The second form of spiritual rebellion makes God into a cosmic cop. The alcoholic believes in God, but because of muddled thinking and unfortunate misguided religious education, she sees God as policeman, judge, jury, and executioner. Much of the alcoholic's spiritual energy is spent trying to hide from God. This spiritual rebel believes in God but dreads the idea of reading Scripture, and won't be dragged to church under any circumstance. Shirley refused to attend the church weddings of any of her four children. In reality, her behaviors are the flip side of what Ted was trying to do. If the alcoholic can't eliminate God from her thinking, she will try to stay off of God's "turf" so he won't notice her.

The third form of rebellion considers God a "go-fer." This alcoholic convinces himself that God is a genie-in-a-Book. If the alcoholic is nice to God and rubs him the right way, then God will grant all his wishes. And what does the active alcoholic wish for? He wishes to drink. He wants an unending supply of alcohol and for everyone to go away so he can drink in peace. He wants every problem to be solved. (And because all his problems are someone else's fault, this usually means that God needs to change all of the people, places, and things in the alcoholic's life.) Most alcoholics living out this third form of rebellion have a detailed daily memo for God, giving him directions on what to do and how to do it. But when God refuses to cooperate—as he usually does—the alcoholic develops a deep resentment, accusing God of not caring, of being indifferent to human hurts, and of toying with lives. So the alcoholic's greatest wish is that God would cooperate.

The alcoholic is capable of great religious devotion. Religious practice, of course, is no indicator of faith. The alcoholic who seeks a genie-type God is probably hoping to buy off God by going to church and other such activities.

Evan was in prison when I met him. Since he wanted to get out of prison, he tried to make me think that he had come to his senses, that he had accepted Christ as Savior, and that he was finally on the upward path. His speech dripped Scripture and pious phrases. He attended prisoner worship services regularly. But when he was denied release on the date he had hoped for, Evan showed his true colors. He openly cursed God and accused him of letting him down. He withheld attendance at church and began to exhibit a frighteningly demonic personality.

When he was finally released, Evan was suddenly changed once again, at least for a short time. Suddenly God was wonderful again, and Evan planned to go to church every Sunday. He never did show up at church, and soon he began sliding back into his alcoholism.

There is a fourth form of spiritual rebellion: open hostility. One night when Ward had been drinking and driving, he hit a bridge abutment and nearly died. He lost part of his jaw and was left badly disfigured. When I saw him after the accident, he said to me, "Just look how much God loves me!" Then he cursed God bitterly and shook his fist in the air.

These forms of rebellion are not unique to the alcoholic, but are characteristic of the sinful human nature. Any person may rebel against God following one of these patterns. However, alcoholism seems to intensify them into an all-consuming preoccupation.

I cannot agree with those who espouse the notion that the substance of alcohol is inherently evil. I believe the evil is not found in the alcohol, but rather in what we do with it. Often the destruction it causes is the result of sinful human activity. Every active alcoholic I know seems to be waging an intense personal war against God. *Spiritus contra spiritum!* I wonder if Jung knew how correct he was. Alcoholism provides a powerful foothold for the Enemy.

My Story

For me, getting and drinking alcohol became the most important activity in my life. Everything else revolved around it. Several problems had to be managed if I was going to be able to drink enough to satisfy my daily addiction.

The first problem was the disapproval of others: my teetotalling wife and her family, the people in the churches I served as minister, and the denominational people who supervised my ministry.

I could not buy alcoholic products locally. I didn't want to be seen entering or leaving liquor stores, nor did I want liquor store personnel to know that I was a minister. When I lived in an urban area, I could drive across town where I would not encounter anyone who knew me. But when I moved to a small farming community in Iowa, it was a different story. A liquor store in a large city 90 miles away was the only place I felt safe. If I ran low on supplies,

I either had to sneak away or manufacture some reason for making the trip. Not having much money and not being able to store a large supply in the parsonage, I spent many hours driving that 90-mile stretch for the sole purpose of buying alcohol. I also manipulated people and often lied to cover up this activity.

I even discovered a young couple in the church who themselves had alcoholic tendencies. We lamented together that the church was so closed to the idea of its pastor drinking. If I got into a bind and needed to drink, I could count on them to get me a bottle.

Shortly after we moved to Iowa, the chairman of the board of elders, who was also an insurance agent in town, offered me an automobile insurance policy. The insurance company gave reduced rates to non-drinkers. He had drawn up the papers and asked for a signature on a form stating that I didn't drink. What was I to do? To keep my ministry, I couldn't refuse to sign the form. But if I did sign the form and had an accident while drinking, my insurance would not cover it. I did what any alcoholic would do: I signed the form to cover up my drinking and hoped I wouldn't have an accident.

I realize now that I was out of control. I was powerless over alcohol, and my life was unmanageable. My ministry in Iowa was not going well. Knowing that things were going to catch up with me, I moved to Pennsylvania after only two years. There my drinking really took off. I had a closer "safe" place to buy and greater opportunity to drink without getting caught. I even built that secret room in the basement of the parsonage where I could store large quantities of alcohol.

By this time, I had convinced my wife that it was all right for me to drink moderate amounts of alcohol. Now I had to make it look as though I were only drinking moderately. So I drank mostly at night. Jean has always been a morning person, and she fades by

9:00 P.M. After she went to bed, I would stay up late. If I'd been sneaking wine from the bottle in the refrigerator, I poured more in so it would appear as though the level in the bottle had gone down only a little (of course it had to look this way even if Jean got up at midnight and went to the kitchen!). I made many silent trips to my basement hideaway, where I refilled the refrigerator bottle from a gallon bottle. Although it seemed as though I had sipped only three or four ounces of wine, in reality I had consumed half a gallon or more.

Then we moved again—to Connecticut, and getting alcohol into the house became a tricky operation. Each week after making some evening pastoral visits or attending a meeting at the church, I would drive thirty minutes to a large discount liquor store in Massachusetts. Back home, I would carry the bags of bottles around to the back of the house under the cover of darkness, climb over the fence into the dog pen, and hide the bags in a dark corner—trying not to let the bottles clink together, of course. Once or twice, I tripped on the fence and dropped the bags. Another time, one of the bags ripped open as I removed it from the car.

After hiding the bottles out back, I would walk around to the front door, go in, and greet my wife. Sometimes she asked me what I had been doing outside, or about the noise. I usually made up some story.

After she was asleep, I would get up "to let the dogs out." Using the walk-out basement door, I would carry my bags into the basement, stash my bottles in various hiding places, and begin my nightly routine of drinking.

When we visited my mother-in-law, I always stashed alcohol in the car and often made up a supply of bloody mary (vodka and tomato juice) to hide in her refrigerator. I worked hard to hide the amount I was drinking, but my mother-in-law and sister-in-law were two people I couldn't fool. They knew I was headed toward alcoholism, and it was difficult for me to convince my wife that they were wrong.

Keeping denominational officials off guard was another problem. Once I was scheduled to travel with a youth ministry director from my denomination's national headquarters to present a series of youth ministry seminars at churches in several Midwest states. I insisted on having private sleeping arrangements every night. I had to have my sleep, I lied, or I would not make the trip. I found ways to get alcohol along the way, and I drank until I was drunk every night. I experienced dreadful hangovers in the morning, and I could not hide my condition. I convinced my traveling companion that I had a bad case of the flu but would continue the trip regardless. When it was over, the seminars had been quite successful, and I was praised for continuing in spite of being sick.

Lack of money was another problem. Jean keeps the books in our family. (I'm glad she does, or we would have been in dire straits.) Today I appreciate her money management, but during my drinking years it was a major problem. I needed money to buy alcohol, but I couldn't let her know how much I was spending. Frankly, I became downright dishonest. I stole money from my own family. When Jean confronted me, I either "forgot" where I had spent money or "didn't know anything" about missing money. I stole money from the church; I took things that I could sell. In short, I did *anything* to get money to buy alcohol.

If I had a wedding or funeral and received an honorarium, I would pocket part or all of it. If the subject came up at home, I told Jean that a minister shouldn't receive money from church members for these pastoral services or I would lie about the amount I had received.

I began to resent all the people who stood in the way of my drinking. I often assailed the throne of heaven, asking God either to change these people or get me away from them. As my depression and spiritual rebellion progressed, I became more and more angry and negative toward the people in my life and toward God himself. As I recall my misbehavior and attitudes, I am mystified at how I could have missed their significance at the time. I was out of touch with reality—totally denying my drinking. If, at that time, a friend of mine had regularly driven half an hour to a town in another state at night to buy ice cream, deposited it into his back yard and then, after his wife went to bed, sneaked it into the basement, where he could devour the entire half gallon, I would have seen this behavior as abnormal. Yet it didn't seem problematic to me that I followed this same routine in buying and drinking alcohol. None of the things I have described here seemed abnormal when I was doing them.

Many alcoholics suffer devastating losses because of their disease. I know men and women who have lost spouses, homes, and good jobs. As I write these lines, I remember a physician who has called me several times over the last year. His wife and young daughter have left him. He was under suspension because he performed a surgery while under the influence of alcohol. His credentials were restored for a probationary period, but he has been drinking again. It is only a matter of time until it becomes known that he has broken his probation by drinking, which will result in the loss of his practice. He still doesn't see what he is doing.

Some alcoholics lose their freedom. They go to jail because of their activities. All alcoholics lose their health to some degree. For some the conditions are reversible, but for others they are not.

I thank God that I have not sustained these kinds of losses. I still have my family. Jean and I are still together, and I never lost a home or a job, although I must confess that I resigned from several churches because I would have been fired sooner or later. I never had a drunk-driving arrest or accident. I never went to jail because of my activities, although it was only because I didn't get caught.

But all of these losses are outward. The inward losses an alcoholic suffers are greater. In that sense, I lost everything. I lost myself, and I lost the Lord Jesus in a haze of alcoholic thinking. I became a shell of a man. I was angry and depressed. I treated Jean and my two children badly and lost my integrity. Instead of providing stability, affection, acceptance, protection, and nurture for my wife and children, I stole from them, resented them, and became totally isolated from them emotionally.

Instead of providing spiritual leadership, spiritual food, and a model of spiritual living for my family and churches, I modeled confusing behavior fueled by alcoholism. I fed people spiritual garbage, and I had little leadership to offer. I was angry with God for calling me into ministry and for not taking these people out of my life so that I could drink as I wished. Half knowing that my drinking was getting out of control, I pleaded with God to help me get through the hangovers and withdrawal and to help me control my drinking.

I had become morally and spiritually bankrupt, and I couldn't even see it. But God did not let go of me!

Notes
1. Vernon, Johnson, *I'll Quit Tomorrow* (San Francisco: Harper and Row, 1980).

5

How Can I Help?

As you probably know from your own experience, alcoholics are hard cases. They lie, steal, and cheat. They are masters of manipulation. They get themselves into trouble and then go out and drink and do the same things over and over. They lose families and possessions and jobs because of their drinking and then turn to the bottle for solace. Some will even call themselves "Christians" while fighting God every step of the way. They seem so hopeless! Can anything be done to help such a person?

The good news is that alcoholics can be helped. With proper treatment, alcoholism can be arrested and held in remission, so take heart. Today there are millions of alcoholics whose disease is in remission. Just as diabetes can be held in check so long as the diabetic takes insulin daily, so alcoholism can yield to the daily application of a tried and tested program of recovery.

51

The problem, however, is in getting your alcoholic friend started on the road of recovery. "I never saw a pampered drunk get sober," says a friend who has now had many years of recovery. In my experience, this statement sets the tone. Alcoholics live in a fantasy world, but it is no wonderland! In their world again, they believe that alcohol is the solution to all problems. Without exception, they will not start down the road of recovery until they have been hit with the devastating insight that most of their problems and pain have been *caused* by their drinking. In every case, alcoholics must create for themselves a crisis great enough to break through their denial. This may sound like a hard-line approach, but nothing else seems to work.

This "tough love" approach runs against the instincts of many of us. For example, a couple (members of my church) used to live on a busy street, and they had a child who insisted on running across the street without regard to oncoming traffic. The child would put his head down and charge across the street like a fullback charging for the touchdown through a row of linebackers. His parents were rightfully concerned. The child's safety was their responsibility. The most reasonable course was to restrict him so that he could not run across the street and to teach him how to cross safely. They had to punish the boy to get his attention.

Supposing I had told these parents, "Let him do it! Let him run across the street whenever he wants to. If he gets hit by a car and lives, perhaps he will stop doing it." They would have been mortified, and I probably would have been unemployed! Not many churches would be tolerant of such pastoral counseling. Yet that is precisely the approach that's necessary in helping the alcoholic get started in recovery.

Hold the crossing-the-street illustration in mind. The natural, loving inclination is to protect the alcoholic from "being hit by the car." We want to teach him or her to "cross the street safely." We try to avert oncoming crises caused by the alcoholic's drinking and to help our friend out of the jams he gets himself into. We try to teach him to drink safely. But there is no safe way to drink. And helping our friend every time he gets into trouble doesn't help him to become responsible.

I include myself in this tendency. I have a young friend who is the same age as my daughter. Coming from a seriously dysfunctional family, she got lost in alcoholism and drug addictions as a teenager. She adopted Jean and me as a second family. Over the years, she has had a difficult time in staying sober. After a few months, she would return to drinking or smoking pot.

One time she began drinking again after nine months of sobriety. Although I should have known better, I tried to rescue her. I tried to get her to stop drinking, and I cut off one crisis after another to protect her. It was one of the stormiest and most troubling periods I have experienced in sobriety, and it was a complete failure. If anything, I probably only helped to delay the onset of her real recovery.

Alcoholics generally don't appreciate and don't respond to efforts to get them to stop drinking. I recently spoke with a man who currently works in the development office of a large educational firm. In his earlier years when he was a heavy drinker, he held a responsible position at a bank. His job took him abroad on business, and his wife often accompanied him on such trips. On these trips, he got the two of them into "messes" as a result of his drinking. On three of these occasions his wife said to him, "Don't you think you're drinking too much?" But instead of being helped by her caring, he rewarded his wife for her love and concern with a week of stony silence.

It may seem uncaring, but it takes a hard-nosed approach to get your alcoholic friend started in recovery. It is scarcely possible to read anything in the field today that disagrees with this approach.

Your friends has to wind up in a traumatic emotional crisis before she will finally make the connection between the problem and the drinking. And this rarely happens as long as she is being protected.

In essence, I am saying that it is best if you *do not try to interfere with the alcoholic's drinking.* I know of hundreds of cases in which alcoholics were coerced to stop drinking. Sooner or later they all resumed their drinking. Alcoholics drink until they are ready to stop, and the motivation to stop has to come from within.

Scolding your friend for drinking is less than useless. Restricting the alcoholic so that he can't drink is futile. Nor will it do any good to throw out the hidden bottles that you find. The difference between the drinking alcoholic and the child who runs across the street is that the child can be controlled and the alcoholic cannot. At its center, this is a *control* issue, and the truth is that the alcoholic is being controlled by alcohol.

It is also important, then, to *let the alcoholic take responsibility for the consequences of his drinking.*

Mary, Mark, and Others

Mary used to make up excuses about her husband's absences from work when his employer called to find out why Mark hadn't shown up. In truth, he was drunk or hung over. Understandably, Mary wanted to protect his employment. If Mark lost his job, the family would lose their only means for support. And no doubt, it would probably be difficult for him to get another job.

Through a local support group, Mary learned that by trying to protect herself and her husband in this manner, she was only delaying Mark's recovery. She was averting the crisis that might lead to recovery. So, although she would be personally affected, she started telling the truth when her husband's employer called.

Predictably, Mark was angry with her. He said it would be her fault if he lost his job. In those moments, Mary realized that one reason she had covered up for him was her own fear of his anger. She learned to stand firm and reply that it would be Mark's own fault if he lost his job. Mark did the drinking; he was the one who was too drunk or hung over to go to work. If he got fired, he had no one else to blame.

Results of this switch in approach were not long in coming. Mark's employer soon called him to his office. There Mark was faced with an ultimatum: get help or get out! He was faced with his attendance record. His job would remain secure if he would enter a treatment center for alcoholism and begin recovery. But if Mark refused treatment or started drinking again, he would lose his job.

Mark came home from the confrontation angry and feeling sorry for himself. "How dare he consider me an alcoholic!" he fumed. He yelled at his wife for causing the problem. He also tried to convince her that it was all a terrible mistake.

But she knew better. Mary kept putting the responsibility back on Mark. In answer to every tirade and whine, she said, "So, what are *you* going to do?"

He finally answered, "What else can I do? I'll have to go into treatment."

While many smaller companies do not have an Employees Assistance Program (EAP), Mark's company did. Having been referred to this department, he called for an appointment with the EAP counselor. There Mark was given a choice. The EAP could make arrangements for admission to a treatment center, or he could choose another accredited center. Mark decided to let them make the arrangements.

At the treatment center, the staff worked to break down Mark's denial. In the third week of treatment, he accepted his alcoholism for the first time. During his stay he was educated about the disease and was directed to Alcoholics Anonymous. Mary and the children took part in several groups, and the entire family met with the counselor regularly. They learned how they had been affected by the alcoholism, and were directed toward Al-Anon and Al-Ateen, counterparts to Alcoholics Anonymous.

Today Mark is recovering. He hasn't had a drink for over a year, attends AA meetings regularly, and just received a promotion and a raise at work.

This was not an easy process for anyone. But Mark came to his "moment of truth" when his job was in jeopardy because of his drinking. Mary had been preventing the crisis inadvertently, but when she changed her approach, the crisis came and the recovery could begin.

Anne has been less successful. Her teenage son is already an alcoholic. Anne recently received a phone call from the police in a southern state. Philip had run away, and the authorities had picked him up. Anne's inclination was to rescue her son, but she told the police, "He got down there by himself—he needs to find his own way home." To herself and to the police she sounded cold and uncaring. Inside, she was terrified that Philip might not come home, but he did—three days later.

Sadly, Philip is still drinking. No one knows when he will have his "moment of truth." Some people never do. Often those who never acknowledge their alcoholism are involved with someone who they have manipulated into protecting them from the consequences of their drinking.

The Prodigal

This tough-love approach reminds me of the parable of the Prodigal Son in Luke 15. Of course, Jesus never said that the younger son was an alcoholic, but much of his behavior is similar. He grew tired of working under his father's thumb. He wanted to party. So he got his share of the family inheritance and left home in search of good times.

Knowing what would probably happen, his father let him go anyway. Predictably the young man "squandered his wealth in wild living" (verse 13). Quite likely, the young man was drinking heavily. When his money was gone, a famine arose, and he began to be in need. The only employment available to him was tending pigs. This was something that ordinarily would have been unthinkable for a young Jewish man. Pigs weren't kosher! And he didn't even get paid. His salary was the opportunity to contend with the pigs for their food.

It was necessary for this young man to come to the crisis of the pig pen before he could have his "moment of truth." Finally he came to his senses, and he decided to make the long trip home—physically, emotionally, and spiritually.

The Pig-Pen Experience

Several years ago I received a phone call from a local treatment center requesting me to visit one of their newly admitted patients. A minister from another state, Tim, was arrested while driving drunk. Tim's "pig-pen experience," or moment of truth, came as he was being led handcuffed before a judge.

My own "pig-pen" experience came in my family room. I suddenly knew that it was over. I was in a great deal of pain, both physical and psychological. I finally understood that drinking was my problem and that if I continued to drink, I would lose everything. The price of continued drinking had become too high for me to pay. But it took a crisis to bring me to my senses.

These crises, or pig-pen experiences, often come as a natural consequence of drinking. But they can also be precipitated through "intervention," a method pioneered by the Johnson Institute. In a planned intervention, many of the significant people in the alcoholic's life gather for a confrontation.

This intervention typically involves the spouse and children, as well as an employer or supervisor, clergy, close friends, and relatives. An intervention leader coaches these significant people in expressing to the alcoholic exactly how his or her drinking is affecting them. Since the alcoholic's friends and loved ones are often as frightened as the alcoholic, the sheer magnitude of the confrontation usually overwhelms the alcoholic, creating a crisis. Instead of waiting for the alcoholic to "hit bottom," the bottom is raised by others to meet the alcoholic on his or her downward slide.

Regardless of how the crisis comes, a pig-pen experience is an opportunity for recovery to begin. But unless some positive action is taken during the crisis, the alcoholic will resolve the situation with more drinking and the moment will be lost.

Two Directions

In my experience, there are two basic directions to go at this point. The first is to get the alcoholic into a treatment program, if at all possible. The second is to get him started in Alcoholics Anonymous.

Treatment Programs

I have already described the course followed by most treatment centers in Mark's story earlier in this chapter. In addition to counseling, treatment centers provide medical supervision of the patient. Medical supervision is especially important during initial detoxification when the alcoholic experiences physical withdrawal from alcohol. Depending on the degree of advancement of the disease, withdrawal can be life-threatening. By the time an alcoholic enters treatment, alcohol has often done physiological damage to many vital organs.

The personal and group counseling that the alcoholic receives is a second advantage to the treatment-center approach. This interaction helps the patient become aware of other problems that need to be solved and starts him on the road to emotional integration.

A third treatment-program advantage is the intense and protected environment. It is virtually impossible for the alcoholic to manipulate people so that he can continue drinking. Temporarily cut off from familiar people and surroundings, the alcoholic is bombarded with the reality and consequences of his drinking problem and with the necessity of deciding to begin recovery. The principles of recovery are also presented clearly.

If you set out to persuade your alcoholic friend to enter a treatment center, *be prepared*. That old Boy Scout motto has been my watchword when dealing with alcohol abusers.

Use the phone book to identify local alcohol treatment centers, alcohol counselors, and alcohol education programs. Visit several, and talk with some of their public relations people. If possible, attend an open meeting. Ask questions about the program, insurance coverage, and admission procedures.

You will quickly form some opinions as to which treatment center is best suited to your friend's situation. Keep the phone numbers and the names of some staff members with you at all times. Maintain contact with some key person. Then, when your friend's crisis experience comes, or the day of intervention arrives, you will be in an educated position to urge him to enter treatment immediately—*that very day*. You never know when that opportunity will open up, or if it will ever occur again. Advance preparation will give you an added measure of control and will help you to take advantage of an opening that could easily slip away.

But what if he refuses to enter treatment? Suppose your friend recognizes his problem with alcohol but insists he can stop drinking without help? This is a typical scenario. *You* know that most alcoholics cannot stop drinking on their own unaided will power, but your friend doesn't know that. If pressing your case for treatment is getting you nowhere, ask your friend to agree to go into treatment if he drinks again. *Then get it in writing!* Write out the promise as a contract between friends, and ask him to sign it. In effect, you are letting your alcoholic friend know that you are not going to be diverted from this important matter, and that you won't forget the agreement. You'll hold him to it.

If your friend refuses to sign the agreement, or will not agree to enter treatment under any circumstances, then he probably isn't ready to quit—it's like false labor! His crisis and moment of truth may still be in the future.

AA

Alcoholics Anonymous is a fellowship of men and women who share their experience, strength, and hope with each other in order to solve their common problem—alcoholism—and help others in the recovery process. AA centers around twelve steps which constitute a program of recovery.

The Twelve Steps were written by Bill Wilson with the help of Dr. Robert Smith ("Dr. Bob," as he came to be known in AA). Wilson was a stock market analyst living in the New York City area, and Dr. Bob was a physician living in Akron, Ohio. Both were hopeless alcoholics whose careers and personal lives were in shambles. Miraculously, they found the way to sobriety and became the co-founders of Alcoholics Anonymous in 1935. Dr. Bob died sober fifteen years later. Bill died in 1971. He, too, never drank again after beginning recovery in 1935.

Together, Bill Wilson and Bob Smith developed the Twelve-Step program which became AA's suggested outline for recovery. The Twelve Steps grew out of the experiences of Bill and Bob and of about a hundred other "hopeless alcoholics," all of whom became sober and responsible citizens. Following are the Twelve Steps as Bill and Bob wrote them:

1—We admitted we were powerless over alcohol—that our lives had become unmanageable.
2—Came to believe that a Power greater than ourselves could restore us to sanity.
3—Made a decision to turn our will and our lives over to the care of God as we understood him.
4—Made a searching and fearless moral inventory of ourselves.
5—Admitted to God, to ourselves, and to another human being the exact nature of our wrongs.
6—Were entirely ready to have God remove all these defects of character.
7—Humbly asked Him to remove our shortcomings.
8—Made a list of all persons we had harmed and became willing to make amends to them all.
9—Made direct amends to such people whenever possible, except when to do so would injure them or others.
10—Continued to take personal inventory and when we were wrong, promptly admitted it.
11—Sought through prayer and meditation to improve our conscious contact with God as we understood Him, praying only for knowledge of His will and power to carry that out.

12—Having had a spiritual awakening as the result of these Steps, we tried to carry this message to alcoholics and to practice these principles in all our affairs.[1]

The Twelve Steps *are reprinted with permission of AA World Services, Inc.*

Bill and Bob were influenced by a number of people as they tried to develop their experiences into a program that would work for others. One of these was Swiss psychologist Carl Jung. As I have already mentioned earlier in this book, Jung told Wilson that each of us has a spiritual thirst for wholeness that can only be obtained through union with God. "The only legitimate way to such an experience is that it happens to you in reality," wrote Jung, "and it can only happen to you when you walk on a path which leads you to a higher understanding . . ."[2] According to Jung, alcoholism and other destructive human behaviors are low-level substitutes in the quest of God.

Another influence in the program's development was William James, a Harvard professor who wrote *The Varieties of Religious Experience*, in which he detailed his research on conversion experiences. James concluded that most truly transforming spiritual experiences are founded on calamity and collapse (a variation of the pig-pen/crisis experience!).

James found three common denominators in his case studies:

1. Each person in his study met utter defeat in some vital area of his or her life.
2. Each individual acknowledged his or her defeat.
3. Each person appealed to a Higher Power for help. Having come to a dead end with seemingly no way out, they began to call out to God for help and a new direction—the direction of God's choosing.

The third major influence was Rev. Samuel Shoemaker, an Episcopal clergyman, and the teachings of the Oxford Movement, a religious movement that flourished early in the twentieth century. These people taught that, although God has made a way open to himself through Christ Jesus, we have clogged the channel between God and ourselves with the consequences of our willfulness and rebellion. The Oxford Groups stressed confession, restitution, and direct guidance from God. Through Christ's redeeming work on the cross, God stands ready to come into our lives to give us the union with himself for which we crave and the help for which we have asked. Being willing to clean up the wreckage we have created and begin character-building is the way to a vital union with God.

The groundwork of the Twelve Steps thus established, the Steps embody biblical principles formulated into a spiritual pathway that will lead the alcoholic to God, and therefore to recovery. It is no exaggeration to say that hundreds of thousands of alcoholics have experienced happy and effective living as a result of following these Steps. The reliability of the Steps has proved itself through the lives of countless "hopeless" alcoholics who have become sober and productive citizens, and through persons with problems other than alcohol who started using the Steps with the same results.

Through focus on the Steps, regular meetings, and the use of a sponsor, recovery is possible for every alcoholic who is willing to follow the program. "If you want what I have, do what I do," is the advice recovering alcoholics give to newcomers.

The old Boy Scout motto "Be prepared" applies to your knowledge of AA as well. Attend some open AA meetings. Use the white pages of the phone book to obtain information; check listings for Alcoholics Anonymous (or AA). A central answering service should be able to supply information about local, open meetings.

When at the meetings, listen! Don't judge all AA groups on the basis of one or two meetings. Every group has its own personality. Pick up a meeting schedule; take home some of the free literature from the rack. Read a couple of books. Talk to people after the meetings. If you are uncomfortable about being called on to share at a meeting, say something like, "Hi. My name is (first name only), and I'm visiting. I'd just like to listen today."

AA often works where nothing else does. Most accredited treatment centers in the country encourage their patients to become involved in AA. With or without treatment, AA is a vital ingredient in lifelong sobriety for the recovering alcoholic.

When that moment of crisis comes, if the alcoholic in your life can't be convinced to enter treatment, urge him to attend some AA meetings. Again, your preparation will put you in control. You will be ready to take your friend to a meeting or to hand him the phone number of someone in one of the groups you attended who has agreed to help.

A Closer Look at AA

In spite of its success record, many Christians are suspicious of AA. One criticism is that it is not specifically a Christian organization. Many believers are alarmed by the vague talk of a Higher Power, which could be anything the alcoholic wants it to be. Others firmly believe that recovery can only begin with a sound conversion experience in which the alcoholic accepts Christ as Savior and Lord. Many are distressed when AA meetings become the alcoholic's "church." I personally continue to be put off by members of AA who speak of prayer, God's will, and closeness with God in one breath, only to use the Name of my Redeemer as a curse in the next.

I believe that AA is not *a-christian,* but rather *pre-christian.* Because of the alcoholic's intense rebellion against God, and because of her muddled thinking, it seems scarcely possible for her to begin with a conversion experience or to name Jesus as the Higher Power. For many alcoholics, especially early in recovery, church attendance is out of the question; the long-ingrained lifestyle characteristics of the alcoholic won't disappear overnight.

AA specifically opens the spiritual door at the only place most sick and suffering alcoholics can enter. As they grow in recovery and begin to grasp the spiritual principles being offered, many alcoholics become Christians. In fact, in my own experience, the recovering alcoholics I know who are Christians possess a depth of spiritual understanding and commitment which far exceeds that of the average church member. Unfortunately too many churches largely dismiss the value of AA.

Alcoholics spend years giving their lives over to the control of alcohol. Their alcoholism takes them places they don't want to go, puts them in circumstances they don't want to be in, and gives them feelings they don't want to have. As a miracle of the grace of God, some of them come to a moment of truth in which they realize that only God can save them from the grip of their alcoholic addiction, and so they turn to God for the help they need.

Your alcoholic friend must learn to stop trying to control her own life. Her primary objective should be to turn her life and will over to God's care. None of this happens instantly or easily, and the program of AA can provide the means by which this transition might occur. Although it is not a Christian program, it helps the alcoholic grow to the point where she can become a Christian.

Admittedly there are many in AA who, though they stay sober, never come to Christ or the church. I have no explanation for this. Since I believe that only God can release the alcoholic from his addiction, it follows that I believe all alcoholics in recovery are miracles of God's grace. It is possible that their spiritual growth is extremely slow, perhaps imperceptible. I have learned not to judge their inner spiritual progress on the basis of visible externals. God loves them, and he is patient with them. I am in no position to mandate where I think they should be.

Many Christians do not understand AA's focus and role. In fact, there are several Christian recovery groups and rehabilitation centers that are distinctly anti-AA. In their literature and presentations, they spend more time telling alcoholics to stay away from AA than they spend on recovery. These groups do not consider alcoholism a disease, but only sin, pure and simple. To recover, one must confess his sin, accept Jesus Christ, and "sin no more." They claim that AA's disease concept hinders recovery because it hides its true nature (sin) and helps the alcoholic avoid responsibility for it. Many also see the Twelve Steps as a tool of the devil. They teach that the Higher Power of AA diverts people from the God of heaven and is, in actuality, Satan himself.

It concerns me when I hear that God isn't the Higher Power of AA. Anyone investigating AA literature will plainly see that the founders of AA are talking about the God of heaven, the Father of Jesus, when they speak of "Higher Power," though it may not be specifically stated. It shakes me deeply when I hear Satan being credited for that which can only be the work of God.

I am concerned about those who teach against an organization that provides help to hurting people. In the Scriptures, a group of opposers leveled a similar claim against Jesus:

Then they brought him a demon-possessed man who was blind and mute, and Jesus healed him, so that he could both talk and see. All the people were astonished and said, "Could this be the Son of David?"

But when the Pharisees heard this, they said, "It is only by Beelzebub, the prince of demons, that this fellow drives out demons."

Jesus knew their thoughts and said to them, "Every kingdom divided against itself will be ruined, and every city or household divided against itself will not stand. If Satan drives out Satan, he is divided against himself. How then can his kingdom stand? And if I drive out demons by Beelzebub, by whom do your people drive them out? So then, they will be your judges. But if I drive out demons by the Spirit of God, then the kingdom of God has come upon you.

"Or again, how can anyone enter a strong man's house and carry off his possessions unless he first ties up the strong man? Then he can rob his house.

"He who is not with me is against me, and he who does not gather with me scatters. And so I tell you, every sin and blasphemy will be forgiven men, but the blasphemy against the Spirit will not be forgiven. Anyone who speaks a word against the Son of Man will be forgiven, but anyone who speaks against the Holy Spirit will not be forgiven, either in this age or in the age to come." Matthew 12:22-32

It is dangerous to credit Satan with the recovery given to an alcoholic by God.

Of course I strongly believe that the recovering alcoholic needs *both* AA and the church. The church doesn't understand alcoholism or recovery for the most part; sometimes, sadly enough, it doesn't understand spirituality too well either. AA, for its part, doesn't understand Christ. Remember that AA has no systematic theology; it was not written by persons who were theologians or even churchmen. It was written by two men who simply tried to capture their own experience in a way that would help others.

67

For the recovering alcoholic, AA provides a program and a forum for dealing with alcoholism, and a set of guidelines that can lead to spiritual growth. The church provides the knowledge of Christ and the means for channeling one's life energies into working for the kingdom of God. Both provide a spiritual community that is vital to the recovering alcoholic.

This book is not intended to be an apologetic for Alcoholics Anonymous. I have written all of this because so many Christians are confused about the program. They want to see their loved ones recover, but they are fearful about what will happen to them spiritually as a result of AA membership. I encourage you not to have mixed feelings about sending your friend off to AA. Later, when the foundation for recovery has been laid, you can encourage your friend to attend a church.

When giving his testimony recently, a recovering alcoholic named Mike said, "I have believed in God all of my life . . . but I didn't know it. I thought I didn't believe in him. Through AA I discovered that I do love God. When that happened, I found a church where I could learn about the God I love. None of this is accidental. God has done these things in my life. I didn't find God; rather, he found me. Sobriety wasn't my idea—neither was spirituality. They are God's gift to me. It took me a long time to be willing to receive them. Now they are my greatest possessions. Thank God for AA and for the church, for these are the channels by which sobriety and spirituality have been given to me."

Pray for Your Friend

My most urgent suggestion is that you *commit your alcoholic friend or family member to God daily,* perhaps several times daily. I have read many volumes on the subject of prayer, but I must confess that I still have much to learn about it. This much I do know: prayer works. In prayer, you can offer feelings, concerns, and praise to God. God is working a grand scheme. You don't know what that plan is, but it can be trusted because God is love. God loves us, but he sometimes allows circumstances that confuse and baffle us. We would like to believe that if everything comes out the way we want it to, this would be the evidence that God loves us, but this simply isn't true. God, acting in his realm, offers recovery to sick and suffering alcoholics according to his own schedule. They, in turn, are free to accept or reject that offer.

At any given time, there are several active alcoholics in my life who were put there by God. I talk to them and make the types of communication and preparation I have suggested in this chapter. But, most importantly, I commit them to God. I ask that God might grant them recovery if it is his will, and I allow God to work in their lives where and when he chooses. Then I allow the alcoholic the right to keep on drinking himself to death, if that is what he chooses. God gave us, his loved ones, the freedom to choose. I can only do the same. The choices my alcoholic friends make often sadden me, but I know that prayer can make a big difference.

Marty was one man who I believed needed to enter a treatment center for his drinking problem. His employer agreed with me, but Marty resisted mightily. I wanted to talk with him about it, but never seemed to have the right opportunity. One Sunday after the worship service I felt an inner urge to approach him, but again no opportunity presented itself. After all, alcoholism isn't the sort of thing you discuss with someone in the greeting line! So I prayed that if God wanted me to talk with the man that morning, God would make the opportunity—and if not, that there would be no opportunity. When I left the church a few minutes later he was standing in the middle of the parking lot alone. There wasn't a person in sight except for him, and there wasn't a car in the parking lot except for his and mine. We talked. Subsequently he went into treatment and hasn't had a drink for several years. That was an obvious answer to prayer!

It doesn't always work that way, however. Another man for whom I have prayed is still drinking. I don't know if he will ever start recovery. But God is responsible for that, and however it comes out, God can be trusted to do the right thing.

So long as God lives—which is forever—and your alcoholic friend is living, there is hope!

Notes

1. Anonymous, *Twelve Steps and Twelve Traditions* (New York: Alcoholics Anonymous World Services, Inc., 1981). Reprinted by permission.

2. Anonymous, *Pass It On* (New York: Alcoholics Anonymous World Services, Inc., 1984), pp. 384. Reprinted by permission.

6

What About Me?

Active alcoholics don't make friends; they take hostages!
If you are married to an alcoholic or are in a relationship with one,
be it romantic or not, you are probably nodding in agreement.
Although you care about the life, health, and well-being of your
friend, you may feel locked away in a captive relationship. Caring
about an alcoholic can be sheer hell. Not only do you have to watch
someone you care about systematically destroy himself, you have
to live with the knowledge that you are being manipulated and used
toward that destructive end.

The emotional and spiritual turmoil of such an existence is more
than enough for any one person. But the burden can become
unbearable when you add the anxiety and pain of a crisis (the
prodigal's pig-pen experience) as the alcoholic's only entrance into
recovery.

The answer to the alcoholic's problem is God. When alcohol is substituted for God in the quest for wholeness, the result is devastating. Once addicted to alcohol spiritually, mentally/emotionally, and physically, only God can break the stranglehold of those addictions. Together with a focus on alcohol education, an open and caring community, and a program of sponsorship, AA's Twelve Steps provide a pathway that will bring your friend into contact with the presence of God through Jesus Christ. When the alcoholic progresses to Step Eleven, he begins to meet God daily through meditation and prayer, Scripture reading, and community with others. The companionship with God and the daily guidance are powerful. The alcoholic can experience a spiritual awakening as a result of following the Steps. A conversion experience becomes possible, and the alcoholic's spiritual thirst can be quenched.

Such a spiritual awakening happened in my case. I spent most of my life fighting God, but today the Spirit of God bubbles up like a fountain, satisfying my deepest needs. Today I am secure in the grace and love of God. His daily guidance has given me something worth doing with my life. And my experience of relationship with God keeps on growing.

As I sat down at the computer to begin this chapter, a man whom I haven't seen in several months stopped by my office. He is a recovering alcoholic. The first thing he said to me was, "Charles, you're different than when I saw you last. You've grown spiritually in here (he pointed to his chest), and it's the most obvious thing about you before you even say a word."

What he senses in me is God's presence. Today drinking alcohol is about the farthest thing from my mind. It's not that I don't think about it, even after many years of sobriety. But I know that I am addicted and that if I take one drink, I will activate the addiction and be dragged down into the pit of depression and manipulation again. I now see in myself an example of what it is like to be close to God. Once having experienced the presence of God, I would never trade that spiritual unity for a drink of alcohol. As Paul wrote to Titus, "the grace of God that brings salvation has appeared to all men. It teaches us to say 'No' to ungodliness and worldly passions, and to live self-controlled, upright and godly lives in this present age" (Titus 2:11-12). The grace of God has taught me to say "No!" to drinking.

If closeness to God is the answer for the alcoholic, it follows that closeness to God is the answer for those who have a relationship with an alcoholic. But coming into intimacy with God is no easier for you than for the alcoholic. Up until now, your focus may have been on your friend or family member and his or her alcoholism. Most of this book has been devoted to helping you understand alcoholism so that you can help that person better. But the truth is that people who have a close relationship with an alcoholic can have a serious problem as well. Professionals call this problem *codependence*.

Codependence

Years ago codependence was thought to appear only in alcoholic relationships. Now we know that codependency appears in any dysfunctional family where there is a primary stressor—someone who constantly puts pressure on others in the home. What does this mean? That the other members of the household adapt to the stress by trying to control it. When the children grow up and leave home, they continue to bring these adaptive patterns into other relationships, including marriage, even though they are no longer necessary. The grown child is no longer living in the distressed environment of early life, yet she continues the survival behavior that was formerly necessary. These patterns were protective in the stressful environment; they become unhealthy and destructive when implemented in normal life.

This means that, while friends or spouses of alcoholics may develop codependence in that relationship, they may have already developed codependence as children and young adults and are merely bringing it into the alcoholic relationship. Those who grew up in alcoholic homes, unless they have received some help with their codependence, only know patterns for relating in a world of alcoholic relationships. They tend to befriend or marry alcoholics—people who would "fit" their adaptive patterns, which, of course, seem normal to them.

Codependence is a confusing issue; let me illustrate. When one alcoholic husband began recovery, his codependent wife, who had never taken a drink in her entire life, became an alcoholic herself. His healing threw off all her known systems of relationship, and she created a brand-new stressor to fill the gap.

In another case, the wife was the alcoholic and the husband was the codependent. Within two years after she began recovery, he had divorced her and married an active alcoholic. He only felt comfortable relating within the alcoholic environment.

Dr. Timmen Cermak says that codependency could be diagnosed as a mixed Personality Disorder.[1] And according to John Bradshaw of the PBS series, "Bradshaw On: The Family," codependence is the loss of one's *inner reality* and an addiction to an *outer reality.*[2] The family stressor (alcoholism) creates an unhealthy outer reality in the home that robs the other family members of their sense of inner selfhood.

Anne Wilson Schaef, an internationally known psychotherapist and author, calls codependency a disease within the addictive process. The following is a list of most of the characteristics of codependency as Schaef presents them. The descriptive statement that accompanies each characteristic is my synopsis of her lengthier description. You will see that there are overlaps between items. Can you find any traces of yourself in these characteristics?

Relationship Addiction
Codependents don't know who they are. They rely almost entirely on people outside of themselves to tell them who they are. They will do almost anything to be in a friendship or romantic relationship where this defining of self can happen, even if the relationship is destructive.

Clinging Relationships
In "clinging" relationships, neither party can survive without the other. There is a perceived security, even though there can be no growth for either individual. Much energy is put into keeping things together, even if there are destructive behaviors involved.

Lack of Boundaries
Codependents literally do not know where they end and others begin. Without boundaries, they sometimes take on the thinking and feelings of those around them. In the case of alcoholism codependency, codependents take on the muddled thinking and negative emotions of the alcoholic friends or family members in their own lives.

Impression Management
Codependents spend their lives trying to figure out what others want them to be, and then take on that role. They believe that if they can become what others want, they will be accepted. It becomes difficult when the codependent is involved with several persons whose demands conflict.

Don't Trust Their Own Perceptions
Codependents tend to dismiss their own perceptions of people or situations unless they are verified by someone else.

Need to Be Indispensable
Codependents get their sense of self-worth by finding and taking care of needy people, and by making themselves indispensable to those people.

Martyrs
Codependents think it is their duty to keep things together, to clean up messes, to take care of people, and to suffer abuse, regardless of personal pain.

Self-Centeredness
Codependents believe that everything that happens to a "significant other" happens because of something they—the codependents—did. They assume the responsibility of making others feel good and of solving their problems, and believe that they can and should fix everything.

Controllers
In behaviors related to self-centeredness, codependents try to control the behaviors of other people and are threatened when someone wants to be in control of their own decisions. They believe that with a little more control they can make things turn out the way they want.

Out of Touch with Their Feelings
Codependents have become so preoccupied with fulfilling others' expectations and fixing others' feelings that they really have no idea how they are feeling themselves.

Denial
Codependents deny the reality of their situations. They believe what they are instructed to believe, even if what they are told doesn't square with reality, and they believe that things are, or will be, the way they want them to be, even if nothing ever changes.

Ill-health
The codependent is so stressed that stress-related illnesses begin to show up sooner or later.[3]

Self-Check

I have briefly outlined alcoholism and have given you some ideas on how to help the alcoholic. The question now at hand is: How can you help yourself? Help yourself by asking, "Am I a codependent?" Just as the alcoholic cannot receive help until she admits and accepts her alcoholism, you cannot get the help you need—if you are a codependent—until you are ready to admit and accept the problem.

Alcoholics need God, but they cannot accept the presence of God until they treat their alcoholism. Codependents need God, too. But they cannot accept God's healing presence until they similarly attack their own set of symptoms. I certainly don't mean a codependent has lost his salvation! But there can be little joy in that salvation while codependency is raging.

It's not up to me to decide whether you are a codependent. You are the only one who can make that judgment. But the following questions may help to guide you in making that decision.

1. When the alcoholic in your life gets into trouble because of his drinking, does he usually turn to you for help?

2. Will you sacrifice your own needs and those of others in your family to help your alcoholic friend?
3. Would you feel guilty and worthless if you responded "no" to the alcoholic's plea for help?
4. Do you partly believe that you, somehow, are responsible for the alcoholic's drinking?
5. Are you afraid of your alcoholic friend's anger?
6. Do you think a lot about how you can get your alcoholic friend to stop drinking?
7. Are you angry when the alcoholic drinks?
8. Do you try to prevent your alcoholic friend or family member from drinking?
9. Do you fear losing the alcoholic from your life?
10. Do you let the alcoholic get away with using you?
11. Are you afraid to state opinions to other people because they might not like you?
12. When you are with other people, do you tend to take on their personalities?
13. Do you resent your alcoholic friend for the demands he makes and for the chaos he brings into your life?
14. Do you ever make excuses for the alcoholic?
15. When the alcoholic drinks, do you feel embarrassed?
16. Have you ever been threatened or abused, either physically or sexually, by your alcoholic friend or by your parents?
17. Was one of your parents an alcoholic or drug addict? Was your father a womanizer? Was either parent a compulsive gambler, overeater, or workaholic?
18. Do you think that you would be happier if only you could get a different job, be married to a different person, live in a different location, or have a nicer home, car, and clothing?
19. Have you ever pretended to your friends that you know someone famous?

20. Do you ever wonder why God isn't doing something to help your alcoholic friend?

If you have answered yes to more than a couple of these questions, the chances are that you are a codependent. If this is a "moment of truth" for you, there are several things that you can do.

How to Respond

My first advice to you is to *reach out to God and ask for help.* By that, I don't mean telling God *how* to help you. We tend to believe that we know the solutions to our problems. We try like crazy to make those solutions come about, and we fail. So we enlist God in our service. We believe that God can do all things, and we believe that he wants us to be happy. Since we believe we have figured out what we need, we boldly prevail upon God to do it for us, to make everything come out the way *we want.* To the contrary—I encourage you to ask for God's help on *his terms.* Maybe a better word for giving the problem over to God is *surrender.*

A second suggestion is to *check out the family programs at the drug and alcohol treatment centers near you.* Almost all treatment centers have programs for family members or close friends of alcoholics. These are not usually as extensive as the alcohol treatment programs. Most, in fact, are no longer than a weekend. But these seminars or group meetings are an excellent way to begin your own recovery. They put you into an environment where alcoholism and codependency are understood, and where you are not alone and isolated with your problem.

My third piece of advice is to *get into a Twelve-Step program of your own.* Al-Anon is probably the best known group, and there is probably a meeting in your area. Call the Al-Anon or Alcoholics

Anonymous number listed in the white pages of your phone book for information.

The Al-Anon program is excellent at helping those who share a close relationship with an active alcoholic. It might teach you to create some semblance of a life under chaotic circumstances. It may also help you implement the suggestions made in the previous chapter. The groups provide an open and caring community that often surpasses groups available in many churches. Al-Anon has helped many people through desperate times in their lives.

But, while Al-Anon is based on the Twelve Steps, there are other groups that, in my opinion, do an even better job of focusing the Steps on the codependent's recovery. One of these is a group known as *Co-Dependents Anonymous*. The address and telephone number of their central office is listed in the resource section of this book. Another group, *ACOA* (Adult Children Of Alcoholics), is also listed in the resource section. While Al-Anon centers around alcoholism, these groups focus more on the codependency problem and less on helping you live with an active alcoholic.

One of my dreams is to see the development of Christian groups that focus on both the Twelve Steps and the Scriptures. Fortunately, some of these are beginning to make an appearance. Such a group, *Friends In Recovery,* has published two books, *The Twelve Steps For Christians,* and *The Twelve Steps, A Spiritual Journey.* The latter is a workbook to be used privately or with a group. These impressive books bring the Twelve Steps back to their biblical base. The workbook contains excellent inventories for most of the Steps. These provide a solid base for addressing and changing codependent patterns. Information for ordering these books is also found in the resource section.

There are many other programs that are primarily the ministry of a local congregation, but their materials are available on request.

WHAT ABOUT ME?

In the resource section, I have supplied names, addresses, and phone numbers of groups whose materials I have read and endorse. Ask your pastor if he has an understanding of addictions. If he does, talk with him about the problems you are encountering with your alcoholic friend. You might ask at open AA meetings if anyone knows of a minister who once struggled with problem drinking but is now in recovery with whom you might talk. You might also discuss the possibility of starting a Christian Twelve-Step Group in your church, or in cooperation with other churches in the area.

Where the Answer Lies

The answer for every human problem, including alcoholism and codependency, is union with God. I can't stress this enough—because it is so true. The greatest satisfaction in life occurs only in union with God. In him we experience love, grace, healing, fellowship, cleansing, and purpose. The Twelve Steps of Alcoholics Anonymous have been used by countless other groups as the framework through which their members might experience the presence of God; only the primary focus is changed from alcohol to whatever problem is being tackled. Bill Wilson himself set the precedent for using the Steps in other forums:

Many people, non-alcoholics, report that as a result of the practice of A.A.'s Twelve Steps, they have been able to meet other difficulties of life. They think that the Twelve Steps can mean more than sobriety for problem drinkers. They see in them a way to happy and effective living for many, alcoholic or not.[4]

Perhaps the best understanding of what the Steps can produce in your life is found in these "Promises":

81

We are going to know a new freedom and a new happiness. We will not regret the past nor wish to shut the door on it. We will come to comprehend the word *serenity* and we will know peace. No matter how far down the scale we have gone, we will see how our experience can benefit others. That feeling of uselessness and self-pity will disappear. We will lose interest in selfish things and gain interest in our fellows. Self-seeking will slip away. Our whole attitude and outlook upon life will change. Fear of people and of economic insecurity will leave us. We will intuitively know how to handle situations which used to baffle us. We will suddenly realize that God is doing for us what we could not do for ourselves.[5]

The Promises *are reprinted by permission of AA World Services, Inc.*

The Steps are not a substitute for the church, for Scripture, or for Jesus Christ. But they have proven to be a God-given means by which Jesus Christ becomes more real, discipleship more joyous, and life more meaningful. Getting involved in a Twelve-Step Program can be the pathway to an unimagined level of faith and spirituality—for you and your alcoholic friend.

Notes

1. Timmen Cermak, *Diagnosing and Treating Co-dependence* (Minneapolis: Johnson Institute, 1986).
2. John Bradshaw, "Bradshaw On: The Family," a PBS series (Deerfield Beach, Fla.: Health Communications, Inc., 1988).
3. Anne Wilson Schaef, *Co-Dependence Misunderstood—Mistreated* (Minneapolis: Winston Press, 1986.)
4. Bill Wilson, *Twelve Steps and Twelve Traditions* (New York: Alcoholics Anonymous World Services, Inc., 1981). Reprinted by permission.
5. *Alcoholics Anonymous* (New York: Alcoholics Anonymous World Services, Inc., 1976). Reprinted by permission.

7

The Journey of Recovery

There is a popular perception that once the alcoholic stops drinking, everything will become immediately wonderful. I thought this myself. I even entertained the idea that God would miraculously renew me instantaneously, and that I would never again have a problem with alcohol. Finally I wanted recovery and serenity, but I didn't have the slightest inkling of how to get it. At best, this is magical thinking. At worst, it is lazy! I admit it—I have never wanted to work for anything; I have always wanted successes handed to me without any effort on my part. That's very human. We all want life to be easy on us—not to have to work hard, or sweat.

But it was not to be. I discovered that recovery from alcoholism *is* a miracle of God, but, in most cases, it isn't an instantaneous miracle. It would be wonderful if every alcoholic could make a trip to the altar and go away completely healed, but it usually doesn't work that way. For the alcoholic and the codependent alike, recovery can be a long and tenuous process. It is also arduous. It requires patience, endurance, faith, and commitment, and it takes lots of time.

Perhaps a good way to illustrate this is by telling the remainder of my story. Again, although the details of my story are unique, the underlying dynamics are typical in the recovery of any alcoholic. They are also typical of recovery from codependence with these differences: that the addiction is to a system of *relating* and not to alcohol, and that codependents do not suffer the physiological damage to the brain suffered by alcoholics.

My Recovery

When I began recovery, I was deeply depressed. I was isolated and angry. For the first six months, I was on an emotional roller coaster. I had regular anxiety attacks. I would try to go to my office, but as soon as I opened the door I would be gripped with panic, and I'd have to go home again. I was also panic stricken every morning when taking a shower. Why was taking a shower such an anxiety-producing activity? Who knows!

I also experienced sleep and eating disorders. I had a difficult time falling asleep. I wandered about the house way into the wee hours of the morning. I might sleep three or four hours—or thirteen or fourteen hours. I stopped eating, lost forty pounds, then gained them back again by eating large portions of butter pecan ice cream topped with maple syrup.

I spent most of the first months of sobriety sitting on the couch in our family room. When Jean came home from work, I'd be in the same place as when she left in the morning. Although I usually cook supper, her question, "What's for supper?" always came as a surprise. I hadn't even thought about supper. I wasn't eating, and it never occurred to me that anyone else would be eating. I was lost in a fog. Needless to say, it was a difficult time for my wife and children. I wondered if my depression would ever end. Four months into sobriety, I saw the first glimmer of change. The chairman of my deacon's board was a recovering alcoholic. He had sensed my problem soon after I arrived as the church's new pastor. He laid the groundwork to make it possible for me to seek him out for help when I was ready. While having breakfast with him one morning, I went on and on about my depression. After I got home to my spot on the couch, I received the insight that there was a difference between depression and feeling sorry for myself. Although I was depressed, and would be for some time to come, there was no call for me to indulge in self pity. The Spirit of God within me seemed to be saying, "Stop feeling sorry for yourself!" I had been told by someone with experience that in spite of the way I felt, I was truly getting better. I wasn't going to die or go insane. He had told me not to take my feelings too seriously and to hang on until the roller coaster slowed down.

The next breakthrough came when I had been sober almost a year. I had started to function but remained deeply depressed, isolated, and angry. I received an invitation to a meeting with Billy Graham who wanted to talk with pastors prior to his crusade in our area that summer. I returned the card saying I would attend. But as the day approached, I was tense with anxiety and anger. I had decided to stay home, but when I got up the morning of the meeting, I changed my mind.

Billy Graham was introduced by Don Morgan, the crusade chairman. "There is someone with us today who needs no introduction," Morgan said. "He is known internationally. His name is a household word. He has had a deep and profound effect in the world, and his name is—Jesus Christ."

At that moment each person in the audience sprang to his feet in applause. A wave of spiritual electricity passed through the room, and I felt it pass through my body. It was a powerful moment.

I had not gone to the meeting with any expectations, but only with excitement about meeting and hearing Billy Graham. Nor did I leave the meeting with any sense of having some personal touch from God. But I left the meeting excited about Graham's message, not aware that anything had happened to me. That night I dreamed about Billy Graham, and when I awoke the next morning, I knew something deep and personal had happened to me without my realizing it.

Up to that point, I had been stuck in my depression. Despite the intense emotional pain of the previous year, I hadn't dared anesthetize my feelings with alcohol as I had done before. I was in a terrible spot, but I believed that the only thing worse would be for me to drink.

The morning after the pastors' meeting with Dr. Graham something was different. My personal healing had begun. There wasn't an instantaneous release from all depression, but its stranglehold on me was broken. I also felt that God had re-anointed my ministry, particularly my preaching, and that I would be used of God in new and powerful ways.

It was almost three years later when I finally emerged above the surface of my depression. It took four years and a miracle of healing for my complete release from depression.

It also took me a long time to let go of the alcohol and drugs, both psychologically and spiritually. I had stopped drinking, but I hung on to my "supplies." I had a large cache and a rationalization for every bottle. I needed the sherry for my stir-fry. What is spaghetti sauce without chianti? Certainly I needed that bottle of "black-strap" rum for Christmas fruit cake. After all, the alcohol is evaporated during cooking, right? Then, of course, I'd need several bottles of whiskey in case my brother-in-law visited. He has only visited us three times in the last thirty years, but he *might*, and I had to be prepared. Et cetera!

A friend who struggled to stay sober himself told me one day that he was concerned about all the booze I kept in the house. I told him that I had no desire to drink it. But after several confrontations, I decided to get rid of *some* of it. Some I *needed* to keep for various reasons, I continued to rationalize.

Then around the time of the meeting with Billy Graham, I was unnerved by a tremendous temptation. From time to time, I had been taken with a powerful compulsion to drink. In one case, I almost drank a bottle of tequila—which I never even liked much! In God's grace and care, in that moment of choosing, I walked away from it. And on another significant occasion, I reached into the refrigerator for a bottle of soda and came out with a bottle of white wine instead. I was shocked; I froze in place. I wanted that wine *very* badly.

God gave me the grace to pick up the telephone, which was difficult to do. My friend Louis had warned me, "Pick up the phone before you pick up the drink!" I called him. He told me to pour the wine down the drain. I couldn't; if I had taken the cork out of that bottle, I would have drunk it. He told me to pack up every bottle I had in the house and bring them over to his place, which I did.

He met me in his driveway. He was shocked at the amount of liquor I had, even after getting rid of half of my supply. We went to his kitchen, where he proceeded to pour the contents of every bottle down the drain. As I watched him, it felt as though he had slit my wrists and my blood was being poured down that kitchen sink! I did not realize that I was still so bonded to alcohol after a year of sobriety. When he finished, he said to me, "Now we are going to get down on our knees and pray that God will relieve you of the compulsion to drink." We did, and God did! Although I have thought about drinking many times since that day, I have never again been seized with that dreaded compulsion.

Soon afterward another minister asked me to read a book that was written for families of alcoholics and drug addicts to assess it for accuracy. Before I had finished the first chapter, which described the euphoric effects of drugs and alcohol, I wanted drugs. I can't drink, but maybe I can do drugs, I thought without reason. Believe it or not, after everything I'd learned about addictions and recovery, my first impulse was to find a cocaine dealer. I had never tried cocaine, but the book's description of the euphoria awakened a powerful desire for it.

I didn't reveal this temptation until several weeks later, over breakfast with a close friend. He has no drug or alcohol problems, but he was aware of mine. As I shared what I had been thinking about, he became upset. "How can you even consider it?!" he exclaimed. "Just when you're getting past your alcohol problem!"

Although I pretended to hear his reasoning, I was still confused inside. I very much wanted the old euphoric feeling. I kept thinking about it! I remembered how during my first pastorate I stole drugs from a hospital pharmacy and how I forged prescriptions for my drug needs. Today I know that I often substituted tranquilizers and narcotic pain relievers for alcohol when it was inconvenient to drink. Having surrendered alcohol to God, I was once again seeking the substitute. I confided my struggle to stay away from drugs with Louis. Although I was making it, the compulsions were powerful. Finally Louis suggested that I enter a treatment program. But I wasn't yet convinced that it was necessary. I wanted to believe I could do drugs again and control them. Specifically, I wanted to try cocaine.

One day I mentioned to a friend my desire to use cocaine. She said, "Sure, Charles, cocaine is *wonderful*. It will take away your pain like that"—she snapped her fingers—"*and so can a gun!*" Her words startled me, and I came close to realizing how desperate I was becoming.

Finally I called a meeting of my deacons and told them about my struggle. Up until this time, the chairman of the board was the only deacon who was aware of my problem. It turned out that few church members had figured out what was happening. I felt surprised and insecure, but each deacon offered acceptance and support. They were aware of the chairman's alcoholism and recovery; he had prepared the others. He advocated a leave of absence for me, and the board of deacons cleared the way for me to spend a month in treatment.

So two years after I stopped drinking I went through a drug and alcohol treatment program. I'm not certain how it was accomplished, but I lost the compulsion to use drugs. I surrendered to this reality: I am an alcoholic and drug addict, and I can *never* drink or use drugs safely. I am in remission, but I am not healed of the addictions. I can control my substance abuse by not taking the first drink or drug, one day at a time. If I don't pick up a bottle or a pill today, I won't start the active addiction again, but if I do, I will. It's as simple as that! It took two years, but pain and struggling taught me that lesson.

After I left treatment, I was a basket case. Jean says that during the several months that followed I was the same way I was during the first six months of sobriety.

My alcohol and drug abuse did physiological damage to my brain. Although there has been some restoration, at times I still lapse into a fog. Sometimes I wonder if it is possible to have blackouts in sobriety. On the other hand, I have come a long way from where I was! It hasn't happened overnight, but it *has* happened.

My recovery hasn't been easy on those close to me. One church leader told me that I was isolated and withdrawn from the people— that even when I was physically present, I still wasn't there. He suggested that I work on it. I didn't, and a year later I found myself facing nine deacons who told me the exact same thing. It took that confrontation to get me started in relating to people again.

Although I had stopped drinking and taking drugs, my spiritual rebellion was extreme. While in treatment, the issue of my work came up with my counselor. I confessed that I didn't want to be in ministry, that I felt overwhelmed by it, and that I wanted to do something else. She examined a list of my duties and the things that were expected of me. She responded, "Of course you feel inadequate. You *are* inadequate! No one could do this job!" It was good to hear that the demands of ministry would be stressful to anyone. We discussed my entrance into the ministry. I'll never forget her words to me: "Charles, you need to stop seeing ministry as a burden and begin to see it as God's gift to you, *which it is.*"

I had difficulty in hearing this. At the beginning of treatment I had been encouraged to start opening up my closed mind. If I would listen, I might hear something that would be key in my struggle for a serene and stable sobriety. They warned me that the difference between making it and not making it is the willingness to try what is suggested, even if I think it's stupid.

So I began to try to thank God daily for calling me into the ministry. I gagged on the words at first, and there were many days when I couldn't get them out. I didn't believe what I was saying, but I disciplined myself to say it anyway.

Two years later I surrendered to God's claim on my life. Until then, I had spent my hours and energy job-hunting, neglecting the work of ministry and the place of my calling. When I received my doctorate, church members were concerned that I would move on to another church and more money. I was embarrassed by their comments. Of course I was planning to move on! But did they have to bring it up?

I shared my frustration with Bill, a man who has come to be a close friend. He responded to my endless tale of woe with, "Charles, why don't you stop trying to give God opportunities? He knows where you are, and he is smart enough to get your attention if he wants you somewhere else. Contract with me not to send out any applications or resumés for three months."

I didn't want to hear Bill's suggestion, but deep within I responded. I did abstain for three months, but started sending out applications again immediately after my "time out."

As I said earlier, I had reached adulthood with the distinct impression that there was something sick and suspect about people who are spiritual or who don't drink. I had substituted alcohol for God. *Spiritus contra spiritum!* When I could no longer find wholeness in drinking or drugs, I struggled with God over my ministry. But I couldn't struggle with my ministry without also struggling with God over my own spiritual life.

It's strange, but in all of my journey through alcoholism, spiritual struggles, and discontent with the ministry, I have never had the slightest doubt about my salvation. Since the day I accepted Jesus Christ as my Savior, I have always known that God loves me and forgives me and that I will spend eternity with him. But I had never surrendered my life to him. I did not have a daily personal walk with the Lord, and I didn't want one. I didn't want to be a spiritual person; I didn't want to be a minister.

Full Surrender

After I stopped drinking, it took *four years* of hard work before I finally surrendered. I worked the Steps as best I could, and I struggled daily with God, pleading with him to let me out of my ministry. But I was finally able to give in when I reached Step

Eleven, which reads: "Sought through prayer and meditation to improve our conscious contact with God as we understood him, praying only for knowledge of his will for us and the power to carry that out."[1]

There was no way that I could have stopped drinking one day and surrendered to God the next. I grew through the Steps and through painful daily struggle up to the point where I could surrender control to God. God was—and still is—very patient with me!

In helping alcoholic friends, we must not deny them the pain of growth. Magic wands and instant miracles would have robbed me of that four-year, pain-filled spiritual journey from *spiritus* to *Spiritum*, from alcohol to God. My journey began the day I surrendered my drinking; I continued by surrendering alcohol and drugs, and finally I was able to surrender myself to God. I said to God, "If you want me in the ministry, O.K.! And if you want me in this church, O.K.! I surrender. I'm tired of fighting. You win!"

Almost immediately after I gave in, the very thing that needed to happen in my church happened. At the time I was pastoring two small, struggling churches of the same denomination and in the same city, only four miles apart. I had always felt they should merge, but there was a deep, antagonist spirit between them. I felt pulled apart by the division, and it burdened my schedule to take charge of two services, two sets of meetings, two agendas, etc. I felt a growing inability to be loyal to either congregation. It seemed like bad stewardship, and I felt neither church would be blessed of God so long as the division continued. But five years of my efforts at a merger had failed.

Within three months of my surrender to God, a groundswell appeared in both churches at the same time. Leaders from each congregation came to me asking for the merger. This was no coincidence. Someone remarked, "Why couldn't this have happened before?"

I started to answer, "Because you people weren't ready," but I had an insight of the truth. "Because I wasn't ready," I replied. Today that church is growing. It is alive and enjoys God's blessing. Most of the people know their pastor is a recovering alcoholic. I speak of it from the pulpit and in our adult discussion group. While I no longer have a compulsion to drink or take drugs, I struggle to grow so that I will never slip back into the dreaded disease. I need the help and support of my congregation, who accepts, loves, encourages, and holds me accountable. This fellowship had eluded me during the decades of rebellion.

Now instead of throwing up every morning, I begin my day kneeling before God. Each day I decide consciously to turn my life over to God. I invite him to walk with me, and I ask for ministry opportunities. I love the work of ministry today. It is God's gift to me.

Now I have no more abnormal depression. Usually I sleep like a baby, and my eating disorders are becoming manageable. I have reached my desired weight and have maintained it. I still struggle, but things are coming together slowly, through God's grace.

My family life is wonderful. Some time ago, Jean looked up at me over our dinner at a local restaurant and said, "After all this time, I feel like our marriage is just blooming. Let's not mess it up anymore." We have been married for nearly thirty years.

Now, instead of pitching into my son Steven when he comes in late, we talk about what kept him, and I've learned some things about my son. On one such occasion, I was comforted—and amazed—by his comment that I was a good model for him.

"In truth, we both know that I haven't been a very good model for you," I responded.

"Yes," he said, "but hopefully all that is changed now." Then he gave me a hug and told me that he loves me. I had never had my children's respect before. Now I do.

Today I have a home, a family who loves me, friends who love me, people whom I love, food to eat, clothing to put on, a place to work for God, and a ministry with deep and eternal purpose. I am grateful that I didn't miss out.

Although I still have troubles—bad attitudes, codependencies of my own—I am learning to accept life on life's terms with the Spirit of God as my Friend and Companion.

For me, the price of drinking keeps going up. Today I am aware that I am addicted to alcohol and many drugs, and that if I drink or take drugs again, I will reactivate that addiction. I could lose my wife and family and home, my ministry and my health. With God in my life, I have no reason or desire to drink. I would have to walk away from him before I could lift the glass to my lips. And losing God is a price that is more than I am willing to pay!

It Takes Time

Of course, not everyone's recovery is the same as mine. My story is probably average. I think it takes four or five years of not drinking or substituting drugs, combined with work on the Twelve Steps, to come into spiritual and emotional stability. Some do it more quickly, some more slowly. My friend Marie has been sober for nearly ten years. But during the five years I have known her, she has seemed stuck in her growth process. Andy, after three decades of sobriety, acts as I did during my first year. I have no explanation for this.

Another man deliberately avoids spiritual growth. He says he wants to keep every character defect he can without drinking. I don't understand his attitude, and I certainly don't covet his recovery. In his ninth year of not drinking, he is still on an emotional roller coaster. So, there are those who stay dry but never make much progress—emotionally or spiritually.

Not drinking is more than half the battle, but the alcoholic's life can become stagnant if he or she does not keep growing. Encouragement by friends and family members like you can be essential to that continued growth.

For the recovering alcoholic there is always the possibility of relapse. I know that I might drink again someday, but I hope I won't! For then, once again, I would be caught in the tight grip of active alcoholism.

I once overheard a conversation between two men who compared notes on how good a drink felt after remaining "dry" for an extended period of time. Addicted to the euphoric feelings, these men continued to look to alcohol to make them feel better. While still in treatment, they were planning to stay dry for an extended period of time so they could drink again and get that warm glow. Didn't it occur to them that after that first warm glow they would be caught in alcoholic drinking again with all its troubles? If drinking was so wonderful, why were they in treatment?

Many people seem to have to prove to themselves that they are alcoholics and that they can't drink safely. They drink thinking, "This time it'll be different." It is unlikely that they can drink again and control it. I don't know any alcoholic who can. Drinking's disastrous results are usually the only way to send home the message.

But in spite of all of the pitfalls, recovery *is* possible. In the words of Bill Wilson,

Rarely have we seen a person fail who has thoroughly followed our path. Those who do not recover are people who cannot or will not completely give themselves to this simple program, usually men and women who are constitutionally incapable of being honest with themselves. There are such unfortunates. They are not at fault; they seem to have been born that way. They are naturally incapable of grasping and developing a manner of living which demands rigorous honesty. Their chances are less than average. There are those, too, who suffer from grave emotional and mental disorders, but many of them do recover if they have the capacity to be honest.[2]

I'm telling you all this to drive this point home: *Recovery takes time.* The alcoholic's recovery takes time, struggle, pain, and hard work, and so will yours as his friend. Sometimes failure will seem imminent, and you and your alcoholic friend will want to slip back into your old addictive and relational patterns. These words from Scripture especially apply to Christians who are struggling with alcoholism and codependence: "Those who endure to the end will overcome."

Recovery won't happen over night. But through trust in God and commitment to the Twelve Steps, it *will* happen. Through the grace of God who loves us, the promises of recovery will be fulfilled, sometimes quickly, sometimes slowly, if we work hard and consistently toward our goal.

Notes

1. Anonymous, *Twelve Steps and Twelve Traditions* (New York: Alcoholics Anonymous World Services, Inc., 1981). Reprinted with permission.
2. Anonymous, *Alcoholics Anonymous* (New York: Alcoholics Anonymous World Services, Inc., 1976), p. 58. Reprinted with permission.

8

End of the Story

Remember Roger and Jillian and Doug and Gayle
from chapters one and two? When Roger's drinking reached crisis
proportions and his job hung in the balance, Jillian began to
consider suicide as a way of escape and a way to punish Roger.
Doug felt trapped in a pattern of Gayle's crises and his rescues.
Let's see how their stories turned out.

Jillian's Story

On that fateful crisis day when Roger's employer called, Jillian did
not commit suicide. Although her situation seemed hopeless, and
death was a tempting solution, Jillian didn't really want to die. In a
moment of desperation, she cried out to God for help. Then she
remembered seeing a newspaper advertisement for a local Al-Anon
group. It appeared regularly, but she had ignored it in the past. Jillian

had been sure Al-Anon wasn't for her. She didn't want to talk about her problems with her friends or anyone else—much less in public. As a young person, she had learned not to air her dirty laundry outside of the family.

But her desperation drove her to search for the ad. She decided to attend a meeting the next day. When Roger got home from work she said nothing to him about her decision or about the phone call from his boss.

At the Al-Anon meeting, she was startled to find Lois, an acquaintance from church. Before she could turn around and escape, Lois made a beeline for her.

Jillian said, "I was afraid I might see someone that I knew. I didn't want anyone to know . . ."

"But Jillian," Lois responded, "I'm here for the same reasons you are."

"You mean Fred has a drinking problem?"

"Yes. I've been hoping you'd show up at an Al-Anon meeting sometime. You're not alone."

Jillian panicked. "You knew? How could you have known?"

"When you have lived with alcoholism as long as I have, it's easy to pick up the signals from someone else," Lois said.

"But you didn't say anything—"

"Because you weren't ready to be approached. I've been praying for you, though."

Jillian felt surprised and relieved that someone else knew and had been praying for her. She and Lois became fast friends. At first, Jillian cried a lot during meetings. She began to phone other women in the group, as well as Lois, for support.

Finally, Roger was fired. But by then Jillian was already learning to detach herself—with love. She still loved Roger, but she knew now that she couldn't stop him from drinking or rescue him from its consequences anymore. Because Roger wasn't working, Jill's new friends urged her to get a job and start taking care of herself. It wasn't long before she was cleaning houses for several "clients." She scraped together some cash from their savings and from the sale of some jewelry and other personal items.

Roger was drinking most of the time, consuming the family savings. So Jillian began to avoid him. Finally, she found an affordable efficiency apartment, and she moved out one day while Roger was away.

Roger never did stop drinking. Eventually he and Jill were divorced, and their home was sold. But with the help of her friends and Al-Anon, Jill was able to get on her feet. Her faith in God was renewed, and she began attending a church where she could make a fresh start. After some training, she now has a responsible position on the staff of an alcoholism treatment center. Through ACOA (Adult Children of Alcoholics), she has resolved many of her codependency issues.

All in all, Jillian feels that she has much to be grateful for today. The life she leads is not what she might have dreamed of and wished for, but Jillian could easily have taken her own life—and then she would have had nothing.

The last time she heard from Roger, he was living on the streets in another city. Even after all they went through in their marriage, she still loves him and prays daily that he might receive the gift of recovery.

Doug's Story

While Doug was still debating what to do about Gayle, she was arrested for drunk driving. One Saturday she had finished showing houses, part of her job as a realtor, and started drinking. When she left the bar, a police officer spotted her erratic driving. She spent the night in jail and appeared before a judge the next morning. The judge suggested that she enter a treatment program. Gayle agreed, and she was taken directly to a rehabilitation center in a neighboring town.

There Gayle was brought face to face with the reality of her problem. She admitted that she was an alcoholic and began recovery.

Doug soon started losing interest in Gayle. He felt hurt and angry because Gayle no longer seemed to need him. She didn't get herself into trouble anymore, and she attended support group meetings every day. He felt left out of her new set of friends. Then Gayle asked Jesus Christ into her life and tried to get Doug to attend a Christian Twelve-Step meeting at one of the local churches. When she told him that she thought it would help him, he replied, "You're the one with the problem—not me!"

Doug abruptly ended the relationship. Within six months, he married a woman who was an active alcoholic.

How Will Your Story End?

You aren't just like Roger or Jillian—or Doug or Gayle. I don't know how your story will end. Only you can write the ending. No matter what your alcoholic friend chooses, the rest of your own story is mostly up to you. While God holds out to you the offer of new life, of his power and presence and help in your struggle to relate effectively to your alcoholic friend or family member, it's up to you to stretch out your hands and take it.

This book goes out with loving prayers for many to receive the gift of recovery. I chose the path of wholeness. It hasn't been easy, but nothing precious and lasting ever is. With all my heart I believe that for you and your friend or family member, all the struggles, the tough love, the seeking will be worth it in the end. I know—I've seen the results in my life. And I'll be journeying right along with you.

Bibliography and Suggested Reading

Anonymous. *Al-Anon Family Groups.* New York: Al-Anon Family Group Headquarters, Inc.,1966, 1973, 1980, 1984.

Anonymous. *Alcoholics Anonymous.* New York: Alcoholics Anonymous World Service, Inc., 1939, 1955, 1976.

Anonymous. *Pass It On.* New York: Alcoholics Anonymous World Service, Inc., 1984.

Anonymous. *Twelve Steps and Twelve Traditions.* New York: Alcoholics Anonymous World Service, Inc., 1952, 1953, 1981.

Beattie, Melody. *Codependent No More.* New York: Harper and Row, 1988.

Bradshaw, John. "Bradshaw On: The Family," a PBS series. Deerfield Beach, Fla.: Health Communications, Inc., 1988.

Cermak, Timmen. *A Primer on Adult Children of Alcoholics.* Deerfield Beach, Fla.: Health Communications, Inc., 1989.

Cermak, Timmen. *Diagnosing and Treating Co-dependence.* Minneapolis: Johnson Institute, 1986.

Dunn, Jerry. *God Is for the Alcoholic.* Chicago: Moody Press, 1965, 1986.

The Family Enablers. Minneapolis: Johnson Institute, 1982.

Helmsfelt, Minirth, Meier, and Hawkins. *Love Is A Choice: Recovery For Co-Dependent Relationships*. Nashville: Nelson Publishers, 1989.

Jellinek, E.M. *The Disease Concept of Alchoholism*. New York: Harper and Row, 1960.

Johnson, Vernon. *I'll Quit Tomorrow*. San Francisco: Harper and Row, 1980.

Lenters, William. *The Freedom We Crave*. Grand Rapids, Mich.: Eerdmans Publishing, 1985.

_____. *Alcohol and Other Drugs*. Grand Rapids, Mich.: CRC Publications, 1988.

_____. *The Church Cares*. Grand Rapids, Mich.: CRC Publications, 1987.

Medical Consequences of Alcoholism. Minneapolis: Johnson Institute, 1982.

Schaef, Anne Wilson. *Co-Dependence Misunderstood—Mistreated*. Minneapolis: Winston Press, 1986.

Spickard, Anderson, M.D. *Dying For A Drink*. Dallas, Tex.: Word Publishing, 1986.

Resources

Each of these sources has many other valuable books, pamphlets, cassettes, films, and videos. You can write to them for further information.

Al-Anon Family Groups
P.O. Box 862
Midtown Station
New York, NY 10018-0862
(212) 302-7240

The Dilemma of the Alcoholic Marriage
Al-Anon Family Groups
One Day at a Time in Al-Anon

Alcoholics Anonymous
P.O. Box 459
Grand Central Station
(212) 686-1100

Alcoholics Anonymous
Pass It On Twelve Steps and Twelve
Traditions

Recovery Publications
1201 Knoxville Street
San Diego, CA 92110
(619) 275-1350

The Twelve Steps for Christians
The Twelve Steps—A Spiritual Journey
(a workbook version)

Johnson Institute
10700 Olson Memorial Hwy.
Minneapolis, MN 55441-6199
(612) 544-4165

Medical Consequences of Alcoholism
The Family Enablers
DATA: Digest of Alcoholism Theory
and Application (quarterly)
The Alcoholism Report (bi-weekly)

The Forum (Al-Anon)
P.O. Box 862
Midtown Station
New York, NY 10018-0862

The AA Grapevine
P.O. Box 1980
Grand Central Station
New York, NY 10163-1980

Occasional reports are available from:

U.S. Department of Health and Human Services
National Institute on Alcohol Abuse and Alcoholism
5600 Fishers Lane
Rockville, Maryland 20857

Catalogs of valuable resources on a wide range of addiction and codependency subjects are available from:

Hazelden Educational Materials Catalog
Pleasant Valley Road
Box 176
Center City, MN 55012-0176
(800) 328-9000   USA outside Minnesota
(800) 257-0070   Minnesota only
(612) 257-4010   Alaska and outside USA

RESOURCES

Parkside Publishing Corporation
205 West Touhy Avenue
Park Ridge, IL 60068
(800) 221-6364   USA outside Illinois
(800) 698-8550   Illinois only

Johnson Institute Publications
10700 Olson Memorial Highway
Minneapolis, MN 55441-6199
(612) 544-4165

Twelve-Step Groups

Alcoholics Anonymous
P.O. Box 459
Grand Central Station
New York, NY 10163
(212) 686-1100

Al-Anon Family Groups
P.O. Box 862
Midtown Station
New York, NY 10018-0862
(212) 302-7240

Co-Dependents Anonymous
P.O. Box 33577
Phoenix, AZ 85067-3577
(602) 277-7991

Liontamers Anonymous
First Evangelical Free Church
2801 North Brea Blvd.
Fullerton, CA 92635
(714) 529-5544

Alcoholics Victorious
International Service Office
c/o Chicago Christian Industrial League
123 South Green Street
Chicago, IL 60607
(312) 421-0588

Adult Children of Alcoholics
Central Service Board
P.O. Box 3216
Torrance, CA 90505
(213) 534-1815

Treatment Centers

Christian Centers:

New Life Treatment Center
P.O. Box 38
Woodstock, MN 56186
(507) 777-4321

New Life Treatment Centers, Inc.
570 Glenneyre, Suite 107
Laguna Beach, CA 92657
(800) 227-5433

Several centers with tracks for drug and alcohol addictions, eating addictions, sexual addictions, and general psychological disorders that focus on the Twelve Steps. Programs for adults and adolescents are available.

A list of accredited treatment facilities is available from:

National Association of Alcoholism
   Treatment Program
2082 Michelson Dr. Suite 200
Irvine, CA 92715
(714) 476-476-8204

PROBLEM DRINKING

National Directory of Alcoholism & Addiction Treatment Programs
(including agencies, services, and community resources)
Published by *Alcoholism and Addiction Magazine*
4959 Commerce Parkway
Cleveland, OH 44128
(216) 464-1210

Printed in the United States
by Baker & Taylor Publisher Services